A BIRD OVER BERLIN

FIRST EDITION
published in 2000 by

WOODFIELD PUBLISHING
Woodfield House, Babsham Lane, Bognor Regis
West Sussex PO21 5EL, England.

ISBN 1-873203-74-8

A Bird
Over
Berlin

TONY BIRD DFC

Woodfield Publishing
BOGNOR REGIS · WEST SUSSEX · ENGLAND

The author in 1944.

Contents

Prologue

Were this a book of fiction, the reader would be justified in dismissing many of the episodes as being too far-fetched and highly improbable, yet everything related here is absolutely true and based upon fact.

Many items can be confirmed from official sources, news items in the *Daily Mail*, *Daily Express* and other newspapers, including the *Supplement to The London Gazette* etc. In addition, I still have my RAF pilot's log book, which records details and dates of the various operations referred to.

My surviving so many 'against all the odds' situations, indicates that perhaps I have a guardian angel somewhere, although if I do, I am sure that I do not deserve it.

Truly, fact can be stranger than fiction.

Tony C. Bird, DFC

61 Squadron

61 Squadron, of which I was proud to be a member, had the distinction of being one of the few squadrons in Bomber Command to have The Victoria Cross awarded to one of its pilots.

Jock Reid was severely injured by a cannon shell while over the target, yet, despite very considerable loss of blood, he somehow managed to fly his Lancaster back to England and make a successful landing.

I participated in the same operation.

For him to have been able to continue flying for over another three hours and then be able to land required a fantastic determination and stamina.

Happily Jock made a good recovery from his ordeal and was pronounced fit some months later. The full story of his VC award is contained in the appendix on page 147.

The translation of the Latin Squadron motto is "Thundering through clear air".

Tony C. Bird DFC

The author, newly qualified as a pilot in 1943.

CHAPTER ONE

Oh to be a pilot...

Looking back, I suppose it all started a year or so before the outbreak of World War II, when we were asked at school to write an essay entitled: 'What I want to do when I grow up'. Without any hesitation, I wrote that I would like to be a pilot in The Royal Air Force. I had only the haziest knowledge of aircraft or the RAF, but was quite sure that it must be wonderful to fly. I vaguely imagined that RAF pilots merely went up for joyrides when they felt so inclined. Wartime reality, however, was to prove somewhat different!

When war broke out in 1939, I applied to join the RAF at the age of 16, only to be told by a kindly Sergeant, "Come back when you're a bit older, Sonny".

I had been quite prepared to lie about my age, but it must have been evident that I had not yet reached the minimum age requirement of 18.

Although I was no more than average at most other subjects in school, my Science Master, Mr Pritchard, had already instilled in me what would become a life-long interest in science and I usually managed to come top of my class in Chemistry, Physics and Biology. Armed with my school reports, I called on the Chief Chemist at The Rubber Research Association which was situated in Croydon where I lived.

Despite the fact that the company had not been looking for additional staff, it was agreed that I could join as a Laboratory Assistant and would be paid 15 shillings per week. This seems a ludicrously small amount by modern standards (75p), but money did go much further then – and I was serving a useful apprenticeship.

At the age of 17, I saw an advertisement in a 'Situations Vacant' column of the *Daily Telegraph* for an 'Assistant Chemist' with a London soap manufacturer. With so many older men being called up for the armed forces, I was offered the vacancy, despite having no formal qualifications. My salary was to be £3 weekly – a 400% increase from my previous wage!

Before the war, the soap firm I joined, had had many labels printed for their products with the words 'contains pure olive oil'. However, because of the war, supplies of olive oil were becoming increasingly scarce, so we used to have a minor ceremony each day as The Chief Chemist sprinkled a few drops of olive oil into a huge vat of soap mixture in order to still justify the labelling!

At roughly this time, I joined the Local Defence Volunteers, later to be renamed the 'Home Guard' with whom I would spend a few hours each evening. As I worked in London, I was attached to the Westminster Regiment, where I found that the vast majority of the other part-time soldiers were too old to join the regular forces whereas I was too young.

The nearest to a uniform that I ever had was an armband with 'LDV' printed on it, and I was probably considered too young to be trusted with a rifle!

On more than one occasion, my squad were detailed to guard the Ministry of Aircraft Production offices, formerly the ICI Building on Millbank. Situated on the flat concrete roof, I had a grandstand view of the bombing of London in 1940.

On one occasion, incendiary bombs dropped on the roof. Armed with buckets of sand, I attempted to smother them, being careful to avoid inhaling the choking sulphurous fumes. In between the drone of the enemy bombers, I could hear the sound of shrapnel landing on the nearby concrete. I was soon ordered below by an officer of First World War vintage, who was concerned for my safety as I had not been issued with a 'tin hat' (steel helmet). The relevance of this little episode will become apparent later.

On another occasion, I was detailed to check that the blackout curtains in the building had been drawn. As it was 7pm in the evening and the staff had long since left, I felt that I had been given this duty merely to give me something to do.

I inspected the toilets on the executive floor and was impressed with the mirrors and black marble lining the walls. Before the war the ICI officials had obviously liked a touch of luxury!

I had decided that my job was indeed futile, when I spotted a chink of light shining from under an office door. Assuming that a light had been left on by mistake, I entered the room without knocking.

I was taken aback to see someone sitting at a large impressive desk. He was engrossed in studying some papers, and looked up in surprise. I apologised for my intrusion, explaining that I had been ordered to check on the blackout curtains.

The official smiled and said with a slight Canadian accent, "I guess I hadn't realised that it was dark outside. We'd better draw the drapes."

I closed the curtains. It was not until later that I was told that I had interrupted Lord Beaverbrook, wartime Minister of Aircraft Production and owner of Beaverbrook Newspapers, including *The Daily Express*.

Arriving for work at the soap works shortly afterwards, I found that the building had received a direct hit from a bomb and was in ruins, leaving me without a job.

However, because of my laboratory experience, I soon obtained new employment at High Duty Alloys of Slough. I became responsible for carrying out spectrographic tests for the correct consistency of works samples of Duralumin aluminium alloy. This was in great demand for use in the aircraft industry due to its strength and lightness.

On my eighteenth birthday, I once again applied to join the RAF and after medical and aptitude tests was accepted for pilot training, being given the choice between 'deferred' or 'immediate' service. The former would have involved my staying at my present job until a vacancy for pilot training occurred, but as I was keen to enlist as quickly as possible I chose immediate service.

After being kitted out and undergoing the mandatory 'square bashing', I was posted to RAF St Eval in Cornwall as a trainee ground gunner. It was here that I experienced my first, strictly unofficial, flight.

I shyly approached a Sergeant pilot in flying gear as he strode out to a waiting Blenheim light bomber, and enquired, "Any chance of a flight, Sarg?" Although his reply was unintelligible, he jerked his thumb in the direction of the aircraft, and taking this for a 'yes', I quickly clambered aboard. A waiting ground crew corporal volunteered the information that my pilot was Polish, with only a limited knowledge of English, and that we were only due to go on a short air test because the aircraft had just undergone servicing after operations the night before.

We headed straight out to sea, just skimming the waves. (It is only when flying so low that one appreciates how fast an aircraft is travelling.) I was later to understand that the reason for flying so low was to prevent interception by enemy radar, but at the time I was ignorant of such matters.

Soon we could see the French coast ahead, and on climbing up to a few thousand feet, I was surprised to see tracer bullets snaking up from the shore batteries towards us. My pilot swerved well away from this hazard, and as he started to head back, he shouted above the noise of the engines what I took to be "Just testing the defences" – but because of the noise and his accent I could not be certain of this. Apart from the noise, I did not have a flying helmet or intercom, so any communication between us was almost impossible. Although very exciting, I had hardly expected to be fired at on my very first flight!

The return flight, also at low level, was uneventful and when we landed, I thanked the pilot profusely. Had my unauthorised flight been witnessed by the control tower staff, I was well aware that we would have both been in trouble, but evidently I had not been seen. It had certainly been some 'air test'!

Sadly, a few nights later, this brave pilot failed to return from a night operation to the same French coastal batteries.

Regularly, from the vantage point of my cliff-top gun post, I would count the number of Blenheim bombers setting out for night operations and later would count the number returning. Almost invariably, fewer returned than had set out.

Quite often, German Dornier bombers would follow the Blenheims back, sometimes to attack them as they attempted to land, and on other occasions to attack the airfield. I found it very difficult to attune my ears to the difference in sound of these aircraft, especially when the engines were not synchronized.

As an untrained ground-gunner, I was only issued with a Lee Enfield rifle, and the chances of hitting an aircraft at night with this single shot weapon was almost nil. The Corporal in charge of our gun post had the use of a water-cooled Lewis machine gun but even this had an effective range of only a few hundred yards.

On one occasion, he fired the thing into the night sky and a German bomber, which had been circling overhead trying to locate the airfield, saw the flash from our gun and promptly flew over to drop a stick of bombs, causing some casualties.

Next day, the Station Routine Orders stated, "All ground gunners are instructed not to open fire until the enemy has committed a hostile act." We took this to mean that we were not to fire until the enemy had actually dropped his bombs for fear of revealing our position.

Fortunately, the RAF Regiment were soon to take over with proper anti-aircraft guns, but not until after I had left.

I was starting to enjoy life at St Eval, having been befriended by a farmer and his wife who used to invite me to their home for meals. They evidently felt sorry for my isolated vigil on the hilltop gun-post with no protection from the bitter winter winds. Despite the extreme cold, we were ordered not to wear our balaclava helmets as they might prevent us from hearing the approach of enemy aircraft.

Occasionally I was able to take a trip into Newquay, but on an airman's pay, opportunities for night-life were severely limited.

At last my posting for pilot training came through.

At the Initial Training Wing (ITW) we were instructed in the Theory of Flight, Air Navigation, Meteorology and allied subjects, but at this stage none of us actually flew or even saw an aircraft.

Surprisingly, quite a high percentage failed to pass this first hurdle, due to a poor grasp of one or more subjects, but those of us who were successful went on to an Elementary Flying School to learn to fly Tiger Moth biplanes.

Although these rather basic aircraft were considered to be almost obsolete back in 1942, it is interesting to note that many are still airworthy and flying regularly today, mainly attached to flying clubs.

My instructor had been a Battle of Britain fighter pilot of Hurricanes and had been posted to Training Command 'for a rest'. His sole ambition was for a posting back to Fighter Command. Perhaps to demonstrate that he had not lost his nerve, he would regularly fly at almost roof-top level above a house where his wife was living until she came into the garden to wave.

All the time that my instructor was flying with me I would loosely keep hold of the dual controls so that when he said, "You are in control," I knew roughly what to do. Without warning, my instructor would occasionally switch off the engine and expect me to land in any suitable field. However, I was to find this training to be of invaluable assistance in the not too distant future.

One day he said, "Right, you can take it up on your own now," and then added, "if you get into any trouble, just let go of everything. It will landed itself!" I shall never forget the sheer exhilaration of that first solo flight and I found myself singing at the top of my voice at this very minor achievement!

Due to a bottleneck in the training programme, I was next sent to No.1 Pupil Pilots Pool at RAF Cliffe Pypard. While awaiting a posting to a Service Flying School on more advanced aircraft, to 'keep my hand in' I continued to fly Tiger Moths with the minimum of further instruction.

One day I was sent up to practise aerobatics at 3,000 feet above the airfield. In concentrating on loops, barrel rolls and similar manoeuvres, I failed to keep an eye on the ground. When I did finally look down, I could only see cloud below obscuring everything. On descending through it, I found that I could no longer see the airfield. I had evidently drifted some distance away from the only landmarks with which I was familiar. I am rather ashamed to have to admit to this episode, but I was quite lost, and with no radio, I had no means of communicating with anyone for help.

I saw another Tiger Moth in the distance, and assuming that it too was from RAF Cliffe Pypard, I decided to follow it. Even on full throttle, I seemed to be hardly gaining on it (trainers were fitted with economy jets to conserve fuel and this restricted their air speed to only about 60 knots, regardless of the throttle setting). When I eventually did get close enough to the other Tiger Moth, I saw to my dismay that it was not from Cliffe Pypard after all; the squadron markings were quite different.

I was rapidly running short of fuel and had to take immediate action. I decided to land somewhere and enquire as to my whereabouts. I chose the first suitable area available, which was a playing field adjacent to a school. I hailed a man and his son who were out walking their dog. Although the man just stared at me as if I had flown in from Mars, the boy was able to tell me in which direction I should fly to reach a town from where I could 'map read' my way back.

Two things happened almost at once. A group of boys from the nearby school started to gather, and for no apparent reason the engine stopped. I climbed out and instructed the lad to whom I had already spoken to switch on the ignition as I swung the propeller. As if he had been performing this as a routine task, the boy flicked the switch at the correct moment, and much to my relief, the engine started first time.

I shouted to the other boys to keep clear, climbed back in and made a quick take off. I looked at the fuel gauge situated above the upper wing and could see the needle registering almost empty. However, armed with the knowledge of the direction in which to fly, I was quite soon back at the airfield. I was some minutes overdue, but I think the Chief Flying Instructor was so relieved to see my safe return that he did not ask any questions.

CHAPTER 2

Liberty Ship to Canada

I had expected to be posted to a Service Flying School on more advanced aircraft in England, but instead I was instructed to proceed to Scotland in order to board a troop ship bound for Canada. There I would receive more advanced training.

On arriving at Greenock, I was surprised to see that I was to cross the Atlantic Ocean in a ship that appeared no larger than the cross-channel steamships I had seen before the war. On 31st March 1942 we embarked in near-freezing weather. The ship was one of the American-built 'Liberty Ships', complete with an all-American crew, supplied by the USA under the 'Lease Lend' arrangement.

The men's toilet consisted of a long narrow room with a two foot wide board running the length of it. At about two foot distances holes had been cut in the board to act as toilet seats, with no partitions of any kind between. The room was empty when I entered and as I sat down to attend to the call of nature. An American seaman came in and, despite the long row of empty spaces, sat down next to me. I was more than embarrassed when he held out a slightly crumpled packet and asked, "Gum chum?"

He was just trying to be friendly.

Because of the cold on leaving Greenock, we were all grateful for our thick issue woollen underwear, roll-neck sweaters and balaclava helmets. Protected in this way against the elements, I situated myself as far for'ard as possible to watch the huge waves breaking over the bows, each one looking as if it would engulf the entire ship. As each wave approached, the ship would rise up almost like a lift, only to plunge down into a trough, when I could only see the next wall of water ahead. I was rather enjoying the experience, when one of the crew ordered me to go below, evidently concerned that I might get washed overboard.

As we were part of a large convoy, our speed was only that of the slowest ship, probably no more than 10 knots. About three days out from Greenock, the weather started to become milder, rather to our surprise.

Soon we discarded our winter clothes as the weather continued to improve. I can remember someone saying, "I thought Canada was a cold place – especially in winter!"

Another passenger with a sextant calculated that we were many miles South of our expected route.

After ten days at sea, we sailed into New York harbour instead of Halifax, Nova Scotia. Due to wartime security, I had to wait until after the war to learn the reason for this. It was at this period of the war that the experts at Bletchley Park had been able to break the secret German enigma code, and it was possible to decrypt messages between the German Naval Admiral and his 'U' Boat Captains.

Through their network of spies, it had become known to the Germans that a large convoy had left Greenock on route for Halifax. U-Boats had been ordered to surround Halifax Bay and await our arrival. With this knowledge, the British Admiralty was able to order a change of route to New York. There must have been many frustrated 'U' boat personnel when we failed to arrive at Halifax.

On arrival at New York we were taken to Grand Central Station, with instructions 'not to go wandering off', as our train was due to leave for Canada next morning. The temptation to see 'The Big Apple' was too great, however. In the company of an airman from Yorkshire, I made my way out of the station and soon found a self-service restaurant. After the rationing in England, it was mouth watering to see so many items available. We piled our trays up with an assortment of food, including apple-pie with real cream. On reaching the checkout and on proffering English pounds, the assistant looked in disdain and said, "We only take real money." He probably did not intend to be rude, but my Yorkshire friend was ready to start a fight at what he considered to be an insult.

Fortunately for international relations, a generous New Yorker slapped down a ten dollar bill and said, "This'll see you boys OK!" He walked off without waiting for any change. In 1942 ten dollars was quite a lot of money and, as our benefactor had only had a coffee, there was some change to come. The cashier was not sure what he should do about this, but my Yorkshire friend held out his hand and said, "We'll take that!" Perhaps realising that he had been only seconds away from a punch on the nose, the cashier passed over the change without argument. It did not amount to very much, but was sufficient for us to buy some oranges on the train journey through the State of Maine the next morning, en route for Canada.

As we made our way back to Grand Central Station at around midnight, we were intrigued to see the whole road dug up and illuminated by floodlights. A huge team of men were engaged in laying either pipework or cables. We were told that by daylight the work would have been completed and people commuting to work in the morning would not even be aware that the road had been dug up. It showed just what could be achieved given the will and the organisation. When people saw our RAF uniforms with the albatross badges, we were sometimes mistaken for Battle of Britain pilots but we had to confess that we were merely pilots in training. We arrived back on the train in plenty of time for the journey North and without our absence having been noticed.

Our immediate destination in Canada was a transit camp at Moncton, New Brunswick, where we were stationed until a posting came through for a Service Flying School. The very first evening in town I was invited for a meal with a Mr and Mrs Steves and their daughter. Their hospitality was almost overwhelming. I was taken with them to their summer vacation residence in Nova Scotia, where we enjoyed many happy hours on their boat cruising along the river.

I stayed there for one full weekend under the impression that no postings would be likely to come through on a Saturday or Sunday. On Monday, when I returned to camp, I was informed that my name had been on a list and that I had missed a posting. I fully expected to be in trouble for having been absent without permission, but for some reason no questions were asked and my name appeared on a further list for posting a few days later.

Nowadays almost everyone would fly for the 2,500 mile journey from New Brunswick to Medicine Hat in Alberta, but I found the long train journey to be unforgettable and certainly a better way of seeing the changing scenery. The huge steam train took the journey in leisurely fashion with long stops at all the principal stations along the route and ample time to look around before proceeding. At each stop a group of First World War Air Force veterans were there to hand out cigarettes and candy. Although we arrived at Winnipeg at 6am, a contingent of veterans were there to greet us as usual.

Our travel was in first class luxury at the expense of the Canadian Government. I had never been very attentive at

The train to Canada from New York – note the 'Mountie'.

28 · A BIRD OVER BERLIN

school during geography lessons and I was therefore amazed to learn that we were not yet half way to our final destination, the distance that we had to travel by land from New Brunswick to Medicine Hat in Alberta exceeding the distance we had sailed across the Atlantic Ocean!

Each evening, after we had retired to our bunks, the Filipino sleeping car attendants would squat on the floor and sing their native songs, accompanied by guitars. It would have been a most romantic experience had there been any girls with us to share it!

Not long after the start of our journey we could see a huge expanse of water to one side of the train, so large that it could have been the sea. We steamed alongside it all night and were surprised to see it was still there next morning. It was Lake Superior. The size of the country through which we were travelling started to dawn on us.

After more than four days, we arrived at Medicine Hat and were taken by road to No.34 Service Flying Training School nearby. That evening I visited the local 'Empire Club' in town which was for the use of service personnel. I had been tinkling on the piano in an amateurish way when a lady tapped me on the shoulder to say that the place would shortly close for the day and would I like to come home with her for a meal – an offer which I gratefully accepted. She had a large house in the better part of town and I was introduced to her husband, Dr McCharles and their daughter Phil.

During the whole of my stay at Medicine Hat the McCharles family treated me with unstinting hospitality and I felt guilty that I had nothing to give them in return. When I was off duty Phil and I became good friends, and the Doctor, who was a leading surgeon in Western Canada, allowed me to drive his Chrysler 'Royal' automatic car. It had such a powerful engine that it seemed to take all the hills happily without changing gear.

At the time I did not have a driving licence, but as I was flying an aeroplane, it was assumed that I could drive a car. On informing my host of this omission, I was taken to the appropriate department where for a fee of one dollar, a licence was promptly issued.

During a night flying exercise when I had been instructed to carry out several circuits of the airfield and practice landings, I was caught in a freak hailstorm and on landing, several holes were found in the fabric covered wings. Hailstones as large as golf balls were not unusual and these could do serious damage to the Airspeed Oxford aircraft we used for training. Part of the training consisted of formation flying with another pupil pilot. The rendezvous area was a large lake nearby. As, at any one time there could be a dozen or more aircraft in the vicinity engaged upon various training exercises, it was agreed that the one with whom I was due to 'format' with would lower his undercarriage so I could recognise him.

After a few minutes of formation flying, the other pilot decided that it would be fun to skim the water of the lake. In his excitement he completely forgot that his undercarriage was still lowered, and although I signalled him to fly higher, he just thought that I was 'chicken' at flying so near the water. I could see the spray from the wheels of his aircraft that were actually just touching the water and, had he gone any lower, the drag would have caused him to crash into the lake. It was not until we had both safely landed that I told him how near to disaster he had been. He was quite shaken to realise this.

The training on the twin engine Airspeed Oxford aircraft included several quite long distance cross-country flights with much greater distances involved compared to the quite short flights which I had carried out on the Tiger Moth aircraft in England. As the airfield at Medicine Hat was nearly 4,000ft above sea level where the air was less dense, certain precautions were necessary before undertaking any such flight. The regulations stipulated that blankets and other emergency equipment had to be carried in case of a forced landing away from base, and this added considerably to the total weight of the aircraft.

All long distance flights had to begin in the cool of the morning, as towards midday the temperature became so high that there would be a danger of the less powerful aircraft being unable to become airborne on the length of runway available. My first solo cross-country flight was to Swift Current, Saskatchewan, another Royal Canadian Air Force base. About half way, one engine failed. As it was not possible to maintain height on only one engine, I had no

When flying in formation on Airspeed Oxford aircraft, although strictly against regulations, I would sometimes hold the control column between my legs so that I could aim my camera out of the window at another aircraft. This is hardly something that should be recommended when flying in formation, but I did manage to get some great photos!

choice but to make a forced landing somewhere in the prairie. Fortunately, the area was fairly flat with few obstructions apart from a few cactus bushes, and I was able to touch down safely.

There was no human habitation for many miles, and it was a strange experience to be so far from possible contact with anyone. We had been told that if we were forced to make an emergency landing we should stay with our aircraft and not to go wandering off anywhere. After my non-arrival at Swift Current, a search plane was sent, together with a mechanic to my rescue. After a wait of only a few hours, an aircraft duly arrived. The mechanic changed the sparking plugs and cleaned the fuel pump which overcame the problem with the engine. With the other aircraft flying alongside, we flew back to base in formation. It was fortunate that I had not strayed off the correct track to Swift Current, or in that vast, featureless expanse I might have faced* a long wait for a rescuer.

A few days later I carried out a second similar flight to Moose Jaw, also in Saskatchewan, this time without mishap. My instructor was keen to see the famous Calgary Stampede and made this an excuse for another cross-country flight. In those days Calgary airport was little more than a grass field with a few huts, very different from today. We were intrigued to watch the cowboys clinging to the horns of the bucking steers almost as if they were glued there. The rider that managed to stay on longest was the winner. There were also amazing exhibitions of lassoing, breaking in wild horses and similar spectacles.

As usual, when I was off duty, I was invited to the home of Dr and Mrs McCharles to relax, away from the airfield. The Doctor, one of the leading surgeons in Western Canada, was one of the least pretentious people I had ever met and had no interest in trying to impress anyone with his importance. On a holiday in England – before the war – he had purchased an Austin 7 car which he used around town to visit his patients, rather than his big six-litre Chrysler Royal automatic.

He often wore a pair of old army boots and disdained to dress formally, much to the despair of his wife. In those days, the road practically ended at the outskirts of town and several times the Doctor took me on visits to patients living way out on the prairie in isolated farmhouses. We needed to steer around cactus bushes and bump over the uneven ground to get there, but always received a hearty welcome on arrival.

Before returning to Medicine Hat, as Calgary is close to the foothills of The Rockies, we flew on further west for some distance. Although the mighty Rocky Mountains were still about thirty miles away, we were able to see them clearly from the vantage point of our aircraft, stretching onwards towards British Columbia.

I had already fallen in love with Canada and had vowed to return one day, but it was to be many years before my wife and I were able to return as tourists. We did not see Medicine Hat, although I am told that the old swing-door saloons that I remembered have all gone and have been replaced with modern bars. We did visit Calgary however and had lunch in the famous revolving restaurant at the top of Calgary Tower. As the restaurant slowly rotated I had to confess that I could not see anything to remind me of my visit in 1942. The high rise office and apartment buildings were more reminiscent of a scaled-down New York. On this occasion, we were able to tour The Rockies and spend some time in Vancouver, in addition to visiting my cousin who lives on Fresh Spring Island, between Vancouver Island and the mainland.

Back at the home of the McCharles family, I commented on the fact that their gas fires were lit all day, despite it being mid-summer and I thought this was rather extravagant. They explained that it was natural gas and that no charge was made for it other than an initial installation payment.

Looking back, as there was natural gas just seeping out of the ground, it should have been apparent that there must be oil below the surface also. In 1942, land only a few miles from the town was only worth a few cents per acre, as it was mostly scrub land and not even fit for grazing cattle. That same land, now that oil has been found, has appreciated in value by many thousands of percent. Regretfully, it did not occur to me to purchase a few acres. When oil was known to be present in appreciable quantities after the war, Great Britain could not afford the capital needed to exploit the area, and it is mainly American investment involved. Some of the homesteaders from outlying farms who sold their land are now millionaires.

When off duty, one of our favourite pastimes was to visit a ranch out on the prairie where, for one dollar, we could have the use of a horse for one hour. The saddles were more like armchairs with a pommel at the front which a nervous rider could cling to. These horses seemed to have had a built-in clock somewhere, because once the hour was up, they would start to head back to the ranch regardless of which way we tugged the reins. However, once out of sight of the ranch it was quite easy to become lost, because the prairie was a rather featureless area, so it was just as well that the horses knew their way home.

Playing cowboys at Medicine Hat, Alberta, 1942.

Some ranch hands tried to teach me the art of lassoing which they made look so easy but which was far more difficult than I had expected.

At last came the big day of the Wings Presentation when Canadian World War I fighter ace William Avery Bishop VC, CB, DSO & bar, MC, DFC handed us our pilot's brevets. The McCharles family were there as was the local press to take photographs. I was now a Sergeant Pilot.

Sadly, a few days later, it was time to say farewell and although there was an opportunity to remain in Canada and become flying instructors, with many regrets nearly all of us elected to return to England.

The author being presented with his pilot's wings by Canadian fighter ace William Avery Bishop VC, CB, DSO & bar, MC, DFC – now an Air Marshal of the RCAF.

The acceleration of the huge steam locomotive was so gradual that although the train had begun to move, I had ample time to finish a farewell telephone call from a platform kiosk to Mrs McCharles before leisurely boarding.

Although we were disappointed not to have been granted the ten days leave enjoyed by previous courses, we were told that the famous Queen Mary liner would be waiting at Halifax to take us home. We were actually given five days leave, but because of the length of time for the journey back to the East coast, it necessitated boarding a train back at once.

On reaching Halifax there was no sign of the *Queen Mary* and we actually returned on the *Athlone Castle* liner. It was not until after the war that I learnt the reason for this. Evidently on approaching Halifax Harbour, a Canadian submarine had suddenly surfaced immediately in the path of the liner causing serious damage to both vessels. The *Queen Mary* was forced to go into dry dock for repairs. Although it would have been nice to have travelled back on the *Queen Mary* rather than the *Athlone Castle*, there was very little to chose between the degree of comfort as both vessels had been converted to troop ships with bunks in close proximity to each other instead of beds. Afar cry from the pampered luxury enjoyed by passengers before the war!

There was much more room to walk around decks compared to a Liberty Ship and we crossed the Atlantic, docking at Southampton, in half the time taken for the outward voyage.

On arrival back in England, we were sent to No. 3 Personnel Reception Centre at Bournemouth where all new pilots were asked to fill in a form indicating their first, second and third choice of aircraft type that they wished to fly. Inspired by the heroes of the Battle of Britain, I had not even considered anything but fighters and I therefore listed 'fighters' for all three choices.

I was called back by a junior officer who insisted that I must put an alternative on the form and I therefore reluctantly put 'fighter bombers' as my third choice.

I do not know what point there was in filling up this form as the die was already cast. The Battle of Britain was now just history and the RAF was intent upon building up its bomber offensive. The fact that I had flown twin engine Airspeed Oxford aircraft in Canada probably clinched the matter.

After further more advanced training on Airspeed Oxfords at No 12 Advanced Flying unit at Grantham including a Beam Approach Course in a 'Link trainer' (an early type of flight simulator) I was posted to No. 29 Operational Training Unit at RAF Luffenham.

CHAPTER 3

Operational at Last

During the train journey to RAF North Luffenham Operational Unit, I met sundry aircrew and well before arrival at our destination, I had obtained a navigator, bomb-aimer, wireless operator and air-gunner, the authorities in their wisdom leaving it largely to individuals to decide by mutual agreement who they wished to fly with.

We were told on arrival "Now you are going to fly 'real' aeroplanes," and these transpired to be twin engine Wellington bombers.

Before the end of our indoctrination on these aircraft, we were deemed to be ready to carry out our first operation over enemy territory, which rather to our disappointment, consisted of a flight to Paris to drop leaflets intended for the Resistance Movement. As it turned out, there was thick cloud over the area and it was impossible for us to be certain how accurate our navigation had been or whether we had 'hit' the designated target.

Next came our 'conversion' to the mighty four engine Lancaster. It was a wonderful tonic for the crew when my instructor ordered me to shut down two engines on one side and we found that the huge aircraft would continue to fly perfectly well on the remaining two engines after adequate trimming of the flying controls. As one of us remarked, "You might be unlucky and have one engine fail, but it would be unlikely for two of these reliable Rolls Royce 'Merlin' engines to pack up... but even then you could still keep going." This thought was marvellous for our morale.

It was here that our compliment was increased to seven by the addition of a flight engineer and a further gunner. When I first saw the complexity of the cockpit instruments in the Lancaster with four engine temperature gauges to check, four oil pressure gauges, and a bewildering array of similar instruments with a multiplicity of fuel gauges ands fuel cocks etc, I was grateful for the services of my flight engineer, as it would have been very difficult to cope with so many things in addition to actually flying the aircraft.

Finally after all this training, we were posted to 61 Squadron, 5 Group, Bomber Command for operational duties from RAF Syerston, near Newark, Nottinghamshire.

Whereas hitherto I had enjoyed a comparatively relaxed and happy-go-lucky atmosphere on every unit where I had been stationed, I now encountered grim, mostly unsmiling faces, all too aware of the uncertainties of life on the squadron.

Close friends were made and lost all too often in a tragically short a space of time. By the end of the war, 2,000 aircrew would die in operations over Germany from the two squadrons (61 and 50) based together here.

It was the custom for newly arrived pilots to begin by flying 'second dickie' or second pilot with an experienced pilot and crew. My first operation over Germany was to Berlin with a certain Pilot Officer Strange, a veteran of some dozen or so operations.

Because of the length of the journey (almost eight hours return at an economical cruising speed of only 180mph) and the fact that Berlin was so heavily defended, a groan went up from the waiting aircrew at briefing when the target was announced. In the weeks ahead, I was to get to know the 'Berlin run' all to well...

As we approached the target, we could see what appeared to be a solid wall of exploding heavy anti-aircraft shells immediately ahead, and it seemed like suicide to continue onwards. It was with great relief that I discovered as we flew right through the puffs of black smoke that they were from shells that had already exploded, and apart from turbulence from the swirling smoke, were quite harmless. It was shells about to explode in our vicinity that were the danger, but there was no way of knowing when and where these might occur.

We were able to avoid the dreaded searchlight fingers probing the sky all around us, and eventually arrived back at our base with nothing worse than some superficial damage from shrapnel from anti-aircraft shells that had exploded some distance away.

After de-briefing and the usual bacon and eggs late supper, I related the experience to my crew who had waited up for my return.

My commission to Pilot Officer had now come through, and although I missed being able to take meals with my crew, who were all Sergeants, I was a frequent visitor to the Sergeants' Mess. Eventually, the Commanding Officer took me aside and tactfully explained that so much of my spare time spent in the Sergeants' Mess was rather 'frowned upon'.

The reason for the subdued expressions of many of my fellow officers quickly became apparent. After each operation, the names of those who had failed to return were posted up in the Flight Room and the following day we would hear on the BBC News Bulletin the number of aircraft who failed to return from the total bomber force. Ten per cent failure to return was commonplace, and it did not require much mathematics to calculate the odds against surviving for the mandatory 'tour of duty' for bomber aircrew – thirty operations. Furthermore, the figures for 'failed to return' did not include many aircraft that limped home badly damaged only to crash on landing, often with fatal results.

My fourth operation with may own crew was once again to "the big city" – Berlin – on the night of 3rd September 1943. As with every operation, the most nerve racking period was the need to fly the aircraft 'straight and level' – not only during the run up to the target but also for a period of time after release of the bombs. This was to ensure that our individual 'target photograph', which was taken automatically, took a clear picture, with the camera pointing directly at the impact point of the bombs. There was great rivalry amongst the crews to come back with the best target photograph.

It was during this time, after dropping our bombs, when it was not possible to weave or alter course in any way, that suddenly an almost invisible master ultra-violet searchlight caught us in its beam.

This master beam controlled a number of normal searchlights, and within a second or two we were fully illuminated in a dazzling searchlight 'cone', and although I was now able to twist and turn, the lights were easily able to keep us in view.

At the 20,000 feet at which we were flying, the searchlight cone was perhaps a hundred yards across and now the flack was bursting perilously close to us.

Suddenly, the flack stopped, but this was not a good sign – it was a signal for the fighters to attack.

Our gunners were still completely blinded by the searchlights and they were quite unable to even see the enemy fighters, let alone fire back at them.

We were soon hit in the port outer engine, despite my intense weaving, and flames quickly appeared from it. Although I was unaware of it at the time, this was a standard method of attack on the part of German fighters for they had been briefed that this particular engine controlled the Lancaster's hydraulics, which in turn operated the gun turrets and the landing gear. Even had our gunners been able to see their targets, with their gun turrets now virtually immobilised, we were literally "sitting ducks"

It was now obvious that my weaving was quite ineffective, and I pushed the control column forward into a near vertical dive and opened the throttles to their maximum extent.

In an effort to keep us in view, the searchlight beams were now pointing almost horizontally but suddenly they gave up as we had passed the limit of their area of responsibility.

'Ken' Kendrick, my Flight Engineer, had already turned off the fuel supply to the stricken engine, and this action plus the violent dive, quickly caused the fire to extinguish, although the engine was now useless.

We had lost about 5,000 feet in the dive and as we would have wasted precious fuel in attempting to climb back to our normal operational height of 20,000 ft, we had little choice but to remain at our present height.

Fortunately the fighters had made no attempt to follow us down and I was lated to realise that they rarely did so. The single engine fighters held only sufficient fuel for about one and a half or two hours flying, and much of that was used up in just climbing up to the operational height of the bomber stream. Had they followed us down, it is probable that they would have had insufficient fuel left to climb back up to attack further bombers.

"Ginger" Lucas, our Navigator, quickly worked out a revised flight plan for the return journey as we were now completely separated from the main bomber stream. Had we encountered any more enemy fighters, we could do nothing to defend our selves from attack, but our luck was in – all the fighters were probably engaged in attacking the returning main bomber stream at 20,000 feet.

Limping along on three engines at a reduced air-speed of 115mph, we were an hour late in reaching our base in Nottinghamshire and had been given up for lost, but our faithful ground crew had stayed up to welcome us back. "We thought we would stay up in case you made it," said one of them, laconically, but the joy and relief on their faces needed no words. We had made it back...

The air battle over Berlin was now starting in earnest and we were destined to complete six missions to the 'big city'.

While awaiting the signal to board our aircraft for an operation some nights later, I had the opportunity of observing the expressions of my colleagues as we lounged in the crew room. Pilot Officer Strange, with whom I had flown on my first operation from the squadron, was sitting alone with a look of great sadness which contrasted with his usual cheerful and out-going nature. It was with great regret that on our return we discovered that he and his crew were listed amongst those missing.

I feel sure that P/O Strange had experienced a strong premonition that he would not return, and I was to treat such premonitions with great respect during the coming weeks.

CHAPTER 4

Miracle Over Hanover

On 22nd September 1943, our sixth mission as a crew, and my seventh as an operational pilot, was to bomb marshalling yards at Hanover.

Shortly before reaching the target we were attacked by two Messerschmit 109 single engine fighters.

I took violent evasive action and our gunners fired with great determination, but once again, the German pilots employed their technique of aiming for the port outer engine so as to render our gun turrets immobile. Soon this engine had been hit and was on fire.

We also sustained severe damage to the elevators and rudders, much of which had been shot away making it almost impossible to keep the aircraft flying in a straight line. Without maximum opposite rudder pedal, the aircraft was swinging dangerously to the left.

As I struggled to regain control, we received two cannon shells in the fuselage, one of which exploded just behind the pilot's position where I was seated.

Although I was saved from serious injury by the armour plated back of my seat, the explosion in such a confined space resulted in my being knocked unconscious, and, although unaware of it at the time, I evidently slumped forward over the control column, causing our Lancaster to go into a steep dive.

Ginger Lucas, our Navigator, quickly assessed the situation and seeing one engine badly on fire, the aircraft diving down out of control and the pilot apparently dead, gave the order for everyone to 'bale out' over the intercom.

Our Bomb-aimer, in the nose of the aircraft, had merely to clip on his chest-type parachute, jettison his escape hatch and parachute safely down, as did Ginger Lucas from the main door further back in the fuselage.

Our Mid-upper gunner had sustained serious injuries to his chest and was attempting to crawl from his gun position along the floor towards the exit door.

Jim Kemish, our Wireless operator, who had been about to bail out also, bravely stopped to assist the gunner to the exit door and make sure that he was able to bail out. This selfless action on Jim's part was to make an incalculable difference to future events.

As Jim was poised at the exit door about to leap out also, he felt the Lancaster start to pull out of the dive, for it was at this moment that I had regained consciousness and was attempting to reassert control of the aircraft.

With great presence of mind, Jim reconnected his intercom and enquired, "Do you still want us to bale out, Tony?"

As I had given no such order, Jim received a most emphatic negative.

"Three of the crew have baled out already" Jim replied, and as this was my first realisation that we were without a Navigator, Bomb-aimer and Gunner. My reply was quite unprintable!

As with our previous encounter with enemy fighters, on this occasion also they made no attempt to follow us down. I have no doubt that seeing our aircraft diving down out of control with an engine on fire, much of the rudder and tail plane shot away and three crew members leaving by parachute, they would have been fully justified in believing that we were doomed.

I was to learn seven months later that those fighter pilots did in fact claim to have destroyed our Lancaster.

Had just one of them followed us down he could hardly have failed to ensure our destruction as we had no gun turrets operable and the aircraft was impossible to manoeuvre.

Our Flight Engineer, Bernard Kendrick, always known on the Squadron as 'Ken', had remained by my side throughout, having ignored the Navigator's order to bale out, though, as he confided in me later, "I was somewhat relieved when you came-to and pulled us out of that dive."

I knew that I could not continue to exert the extreme pressure on the starboard rudder pedal to prevent the aircraft veering to the left for much longer when Ken came to my rescue by jamming a metal handle across the pedal to hold it in its maximum forward position. The handle was normally used for winding down the landing gear if the hydraulics failed.

For the first time I was able to relax slightly and we could now see the target ahead, clearly illuminated by the incendiary and high explosive bombs which the main bomber force had dropped minutes before.

Although it would have been more prudent to abandon all thoughts of carrying on to the target, it seemed a shame to have got so far only to fail at the last moment ... and we had to dispose of our bombs in any case.

It was with some trepidation that we agreed to carry on for the further ten minutes required to reach the target. Glancing down at the altimeter, I realised that we had dived down to 10,000 feet – half our intended operational altitude.

Despite our problems, we were amused to see the AA gunfire, which had stopped minutes earlier, open up again but the shells bursting harmlessly up at about 20,000 feet, the ground gunners evidently not realising that we were flying so much lower than this.

Our normal plan was to saturate the defences by sending in the maximum number of bombers in the shortest possible time, so the German ground gunners were forced to resort to sending up a "box barrage" in the general path of the bomber stream rather than attempt to fire at any particular aircraft. This is precisely what they were now doing, presumably in the expectation that we were the first of another wave of bombers to attack the target. No doubt things were badly disorganised and communications not up to their usual high level of efficiency.

As we had no bomb-aimer, we jettisoned our bombs over the centre of the blazing inferno and were grateful to fly over the area without encountering any more fighters

However, the chances of us getting back to England with no navigator and the aircraft almost impossible to manoeuvre seemed remote, especially as we were already lost, although I had turned in a westerly direction, roughly in the direction of England. Furthermore, we were all suffering from the extreme cold due to a sub zero stream of air rushing through the fuselage from the gaping hole in the nose where the bomb-aimer had jettisoned his escape hatch.

The 'lapse rate' or temperature reduction with altitude is roughly 1.5 degrees centigade per 1,000 feet, so although it was bitterly cold at 10,000 feet, it would have been very much worse at 20,000 feet, although this was little consolation.

Jim started to take radio bearings of known transmitters in England, and by drawing the reciprical on his chart, he was able to obtain a position line along which we were flying. Where three position lines from three different radio stations crossed, gave our approximate position, from which Jim was able to give me headings to steer.

Such calculations were normally the province of the navigator, but our wireless operator performed the task in masterly fashion and I was grateful that his training had included some basic navigation.

Soon we could see the North Sea ahead, and apart from some inaccurate flak as we crossed the enemy coast, we were in comparative safety.

For the first time, Jim was able to break radio silence to request the Medium Direction Finding specialists to plot our position and give us revised headings to eventually brings us back to our airfield in Linconshire.

As we approached the English coast, we were momentarilly fired on by own anti-aircraft guns. We had forgotten to switch on our IFF (Identification Friend or Foe) signal! Almost immediately that we did so the firing stopped. The IFF radio automatically transmitted a coded proof of identity signal but, for obvious reasons, was switched off while over enemy territory.

At last we could see the runway lights of our airfield ahead and they had never looked so beautiful! Once again they had been switched on for our benefit, the main force having landed some time earlier.

Ken had removed the handle from the rudder pedal and was now using it to wind down the landing gear. I found by using both feet on the starboard rudder pedal, I could keep the Lancaster lined up on the runway, and as was standard practice, Ken called out the airspeed every few seconds so as to allow me to keep my eyes on the runway. As it was impossible to make a right turn, I deliberately kept slightly to the right of the runway in the knowledge that any slight relaxing of pressure on the pedal would cause us to veer to the left if necessary.

My landing was only mediocre, and I felt that I did not deserve the lavish praise which the crew gave me, but I knew that they were grateful to be just down in one piece.

As we entered the debriefing room, the Station Commanding Officer, who was probably anxious to get to bed, enquired irritably to know why the remaining members of our crew were not with us – he was rather a disciplinarian and took a poor view of any stragglers who kept him waiting.

However, the reaction to the night's events had now set in and I replied, "They jumped out of Hanover," and continued walking to the waiting Debriefing Offcer, leaving the Group Captain momentarilly at a loss for words.

Eventually he came over to me and asked "Did you mean that?" I assured him that I had not been joking and although he said very little else at the time, the very next day he recommended me for the immediate award of the Distinguished Flying Cross, and the four remaining crew the DFM.

It was not until debriefing that I realised that Harry Aspinall, our Rear-gunner, had sustained severe frostbite to his hands, but although in geat pain throughout the return journey, he had not once complained. As an indication of just how cold it was in the rear gun turret, Harry wore an electrically heated "Teddy bear" suit under his flying overalls and we all wore three layers of gloves: silk next to the skin, followed by woollen gloves and finally stout leather zip-up gauntlets. Despite all this protection, Harry's hands were in quite a bad way.

When the cannon shell exploded, knocking me out, a splinter of metal had injured Ken in the back of his head but fortunately his leather flying helmet saved him from more serious injury.

Of the four of us who made it back to England, Jim was the only one not to have received any injury.

He later mentioned that had I been one second later in regaining consciousness and pulling out of the dive, he would have followed the navigator's instruction and baled out.

It is quite certain that without Jim's expertise with the loop aerial in plotting our approximate position, and later his ability to contact the MF Direction Finding people to guide us on the final part of journey, we could not possibly have even reached England, let alone our own base.

As far as I am aware, no other bomber crew bombed the target without a bomb-aimer and then returned from the depths of Germany with a crippled aircraft and no Navigator.

On the night of this episode, my Aunt had a vivid dream in which she saw my aircraft being shot down in flames. While she did not wish to alarm my Mother, she felt compelled to enquuire if she had any news from or of me. The two sisters were very close to each other. Eventually my Aunt related her dream, but insisted that she felt that I was somehow still alive. My Mother contacted my Squadron, but due to wartime security merely received a telegam from the CO stating, "P/O Bird alive and well."

It was not until she read details of the event in the *Daily Express* that she learned something of the truth.

Some of the crew posing in front of our damaged Lancaster. The large piece missing from the tailplane goes some way to explaining why the aircraft was so difficult to fly!

THIRD SUPPLEMENT
TO
The London Gazette
Of FRIDAY, the 22nd of OCTOBER, 1943
Published by Authority
Registered as a newspaper

Distinguished Flying Cross.

Pilot Officer Anthony BIRD (155025), Royal Air Force Volunteer Reserve, No. 61 Squadron.

Distinguished Flying Medal.

101769 Sergeant Harry ASPINALL, Royal Air Force Volunteer Reserve, No. 61 Squadron.
214631 Sergeant Edward James KEMISH, Royal Air Force Volunteer Reserve, No. 61 Squadron.
388233 Sergeant Bernard KENDRICK, Royal Air Force Volunteer Reserve. No. 61 Squadron.

This officer and airmen were pilot, air gunner, wireless operator and flight engineer respectively of an aircraft detailed to attack Hanover one night in September, 1943. When approaching the target, the aircraft was illuminated by searchlights and immediately attacked by 3 fighters. Sergeant Aspinall resolutely attempted to drive off the attackers but the bomber was repeatedly hit by the fighters' bullets. One engine was set on fire and rendered useless, while other damage was sustained. The aircraft went into a steep dive but, by a strenuous effort, Pilot Officer Bird succeeded in regaining control being assisted by Sergeants Kemish and Kendrick who acted with great promptitude. Having evaded the hostile aircraft, Pilot Officer Bird went on to the target and released his bombs, afterwards flying the damaged bomber to base. This pilot displayed superb skill, great courage and determination. Throughout the return flight his efforts were well supported by his comrades who did everything possible to assist. Their exemplary conduct was worthy of the highest praise.

Above is a copy of the Supplement to The London Gazette giving brief details of the episode in which we lost three of the crew. The paper was readily available in many neutral countries such as Spain, Portugal, or Switzerland, etc, and it was to be of vital significance to me some six month later.

WOUNDED, BUT WENT ON TO BOMB TARGET

Then Made Successful Crash Landing

PILOT OFFICER ANTHONY (TONY) BIRD, of Kingscote-road, Addiscombe, an old boy of Selhurst Grammar School, has been awarded the Distinguished Flying Cross.

Aged 20, Pilot Officer Bird has numerous operational flights to his credit. In one recent big raid over Germany he was shot up twice and knocked unconscious for a time.

PILOT OFFICER A. BIRD

When he recovered he went on to bomb the target. He brought home his Lancaster and those of his crew who had not baled out and made a successful crash landing. This remarkable feat was performed without a navigator. Members of the crew were awarded the D.F.M.

Pilot Officer Bird volunteered for the R.A.F. in 1941 and gained his "wings" in Canada in 1942. After distinguished conduct in one raid he was congratulated by his Commanding Officer and later given a commission.

PLANE TWICE BADLY DAMAGED

Pilot Officer Who Went On To Bomb

PILOT OFF. ANTHONY (TONY) BIRD, of Kingscote Road, Addiscombe, an old Selhurst Grammar School boy, has been granted the immediate award of the D.F.C. He has engaged in a number of operational flights, and after being twice badly damaged in one of the recent big raids on Germany and knocked unconscious for a time, went on to bomb his target. He then brought back his Lancaster (without a navigator) and those of his crew who had not baled out, and made a success-

P.-O. Bird

ful crash landing. The remainder of the crew were awarded the D.F.M.

P.-O. Bird is 20 years of age, and after a previous raid had been congratulated by his C.O. and given a commission. He volunteered for the R.A.F. in 1941 and gained his wings in Canada in 1942.

"Unconscious Pilot" Went On To Hit Target

Twenty-year-old Pilot Officer Anthony Bird, of Kingscote-road, Addiscombe, who has been awarded the D.F.C., was shot up twice in a recent raid over Germany, and was unconscious for a time.

When he recovered he went on to bomb his target.

He brought home his damaged Lancaster and those of the crew who had not baled out, and he made a successful crash landing. He performed this feat without a navigator.

Members of the crew have been awarded the D.F.M.

Pilot Officer Bird

Pilot Officer Bird volunteered for the R.A.F. in 1941, and gained his wings in Canada. He is an old boy of Selhurst Grammar School, Croydon.

R. A. F. Syerston

YEAR 1943 MONTH DATE	AIRCRAFT Type	No.	PILOT, OR 1ST PILOT	2ND PILOT, PUPIL OR PASSENGER	DUTY (INCLUDING RESULTS AND REMARKS)
—	—	—	—	—	—— TOTALS BROUGHT FORWARD
	POSTED TO 61 SQUADRON.			SYERSTON	21·8·43.
AUGUST 22	LANCASTER.I.	W4198	SELF	CREW	BULLSEYE
23	LANCASTER III	W4279	SGT. STRANDE	SELF	BERLIN. 18,000'.
24		JA874	SELF	CREW	X. COUNTRY.
24		JA874	SELF	CREW	To SWINDERBY & RETURN.
27		E6718	SELF	CREW	N.F.T. MONICA TRAINING.
27		E6718	SELF	CREW	NÜREMBURG. 20,000' B.L. 9100 lbs
30		JB137	SELF	CREW	OPS. MUNCHEN GLADBACH 20,000' B.L. 9300 lbs.

~~Paul L. Forsyth~~ O.C. 'A' FLT.

.... O.C. 61 SQD.

Summary for AUGUST 1943
Unit 61 SQD.
Date 1·9·43
Signature ~~Bill~~

Aircraft Types
1. LANCASTER I & III
2.
3.
4.

B.L. 8250 lbs back via Denmark

SEPTEMBER 3	LANCASTER I	W4900	SELF	CREW	OPS. BERLIN. 15000 on 3 engines.
3	III	JB137	SELF	CREW	BOMBING.
5	I	W4900	SELF	CREW	N.F.T.
5	I	W4900	SELF	CREW	OPS. MANHEIM. 20,000'.
18	III	LM359	SELF	P/O WALKER + CREW / CREW	To WARBOYS & RETURN
21	III	JB138	SELF	CREW	BOMBING.
22	III	JB137	SELF	CREW	OPS. HANOVER. back on 3 engines. 3 attacks by e/a. Awarded Distinguished Flying Cross.

~~G.E.A. William~~ O.C. 'A' FLT.

~~E.R. Dennis~~ O.C. 61 SQD.

Summary for SEPTEMBER 1943
Unit 61 SQD.
Date 1·10·43.
Signature ~~Bill~~

Aircraft Types
1. LANCASTER I & III
2.
3.
4.

GRAND TOTAL [Cols. (1) to (10)]
1493 Hrs. 00 Mins.

TOTALS CARRIED FORWARD

A page from my pilot's log book, recording the incident over Berlin.

CHAPTER FIVE

The 'Big City'

The air battle against Berlin was now at its peak and after we had completed six Berlin operations as a crew, British Movietone News came to the Squadron and took a short newsreel featuring us.

When my Mother saw the newsreel at her local cinema, she apparently cried out in her excitement, "That's my Tony!" no doubt to the surprise of the surrounding audience.

There is a slight difference between the two stills which had a second or two time lapse between them.

Following our rather traumatic operation to Hanover, we were granted ten days leave, and it was agreed that a pilot and his crew should be permitted to take me as a passenger. We landed at a US bomber base, where the Americans' hospitality included taking me by jeep all the way to Cockfosters, the terminus of the Northern underground line. From here I was easily able to get to central London and on to my home in Croydon.

Two stills from the author's appearance in a 1944 Newsreel.

On returning to the Squadron, before we could be eligible to undertake any further operations, we needed to find three replacement crew members: navigator, Bomb-aimer and Mid-upper gunner.

We were particularly fortunate with the Navigator allotted to us, Flying Officer Davis, a veteran of more than a dozen operations. He was universally known as 'Lucky' Davis, because he had survived returning from an operation in a badly damaged Lancaster which crashed on landing killing all the crew – with the exception of Lucky who walked away, miraculously unhurt.

Before the war Lucky had been a schoolmaster and was quite an academic type, and being older than the rest of the crew, had to suffer being called "Daddy" – although he was no more than ten years older than the others.

We were more than happy with our new Bomb-aimer and Gunner also, and a close bond soon formed between the seven of us.

I was the proud owner of a 1932 vintage Singer Le Mans sports car, and although only designed for four occupants, we somehow managed to accommodate all seven of us, by some sitting on the laps of the others. The car took this extra weight without any problems, and despite fuel rationing, we managed to drive into nearby Lincoln on a

Above: my replacement crew, including th aptly named 'Lucky' Davis.
Below, Pilot Officer A. Bird, posing next to the rear turret of a Stirling.

TZ: RAF OUT AGAIN

All Europe Off the Air Last Night

U.S. Urges French to Hand Over in Lebanon

'Full Freedom'

THE United States Government has urged the French Committee of National Liberation to give Lebanon full independence.

Mr. Cordell Hull, Secretary of State, announced this yesterday in Washington. He added that Dr. George Wadsworth, American representative in Beirut, has been sent to French Committee H.Q. with representations from the United States.

Reports from Algiers last night said that a solution of the Lebanon crisis is nearer.

The Lebanese Premier and Cabinet, it was stated, may be released soon, "but are not likely to be reinstated in office, for the time being, at least."

British Friendship

Earlier, the suggestion that the Lebanon problem is a Franco-British and not a Franco-Lebanese affair was made by an Algiers spokesman for the French.

He said : "If it had been merely a Franco-Lebanese affair it would have been easy to solve, but we value British friendship."

In Beirut itself new moves are expected following the arrival of Mr. Richard Casey, British Minister of State in the Middle East.

General Catroux, however, has indicated that he does not wish British intervention.

He said yesterday : "British interference in the Lebanon should be confined to purely military affairs or matters relating to military affairs, leaving France to deal with the political situation, which is purely a Franco-Lebanese question.

"I want nothing better than to behave as a good ally and co-operate with the British but, as a Frenchman I must see to the interests of my country.

"Unless there is mutual confidence between Britain and France, the Lebanese might try to play one against the other."—B.U.P. and Reuter.

BERLIN HIT BY 350 'COOKIES'

And this was Hamburg

MUCH of Berlin looks like this to-day. For this is Hamburg, one of the worst blitzed cities in the world. Air photographs have told the story of the vast devastation caused in the great R.A.F. and U.S. raids. But a ground picture brings home with even greater force the extent of the havoc. This street—a few derelict walls and rubble are all that are left—is typical of the battered, burned city. Another picture in the BACK Page.

By Daily Mail Air Reporter

WAVES of Britain's biggest bombers streamed out towards Europe last night less than 24 hours after the R.A.F. had sent its greatest-ever force of heavy bombers to launch its first twin "thunderbolt" assault with Berlin and Ludwigshaven as the targets.

Over the south-east coast the procession of planes, starting early, took close on three-quarters of an hour to cross.

The size and direction of the force indicated another big raid on Germany. All over Europe

Forts Bomb Germany Unopposed

Daylight Raid

NOT one enemy fighter met a force of U.S. Flying Fortresses which flew in daylight yesterday to bomb targets in Western Germany.

The bombers, strongly escorted by Thunderbolt fighters, were troubled more by the temperature, which fell to minus 45 degrees.

All the planes returned safely.

"It was as quiet as a Sunday afternoon by the fire," said one Fortress pilot.

Another said : "It was easy—nothing to it. I saw a few bursts of flak, but not a German fighter in

A newspaper reports on the activities of Bomber Command.

number of occasions, somewhat to the amazement of the local population.

On 16th. November 1943, 61 Squadron moved from RAF Syereston to RAF Skellingthorpe and in the confusion of moving 'lock stock and barrel' that my seat-type pilot's parachute became lost and I was issued with a chest-type. The seat-type acted as a cushion and was fixed via a harness to the wearer throughout every flight, but the chest-type was normally stored at the side of the fuselage, only being clipped on in an emergency. The significance of this will become apparent later.

Skellingthorpe was in such close proximity to RAF Woodhall Spa that we were ordered at night to circuit our airfield at 800ft instead of the usual 1,000ft whilst the pilots from Woodhall Spa made their circuits at 1,200ft.

When we were not on operations, we occasionally visited Woodhall Spa, where the famous Wing Commander Leonard Cheshire was Squadron Commander. On one such visit, some American officers from a nearby airfield had also been invited for a few drinks and to compare tactics.

One rather boastful young American pilot was telling anyone who would listen that he had now completed six missions over Germany and he appeared to think that this was something of a record. He turned to Cheshire who had been leaning against the bar listening politely and enquired, "And how many missions have you done Sir?" Cheshire thought for a moment and then said, "Let me see, I think it must be over a hundred by now..."

The young American was effectively silenced and gazed at Cheshire in awe and wonderment.

A few short weeks later, 61 Squadron plus a small bomber force from a few other chosen squadrons was to fly on a special operation with Cheshire flying in a Mosquito aircraft to guide us to the target.

De Haviland Mosquito.

CHAPTER 6

Toulouse with Cheshire

On 10th March 1944, we abandoned our usual high-level approach to bomb Chateauroux in France at 7,800 feet, and we all agreed that this made a pleasant change from attacking heavily defended German targets, for on this occasion, the gunfire was of only a 'token' nature and far from accurate. As we approached the target, it stopped altogether – the gunners had probably decided to take shelter.

On 5th April 1944, we had a special briefing in which we were shown photographs taken by high flying Mosquito aircraft of a Junkers 88 factory at Toulouse. The Junkers 88 had become our most feared enemy fighter with its highly efficient radar and capability of remaining in the air for far longer than the single engine fighters.

We were briefed to fly at 12,500 feet and were told that the legendary Wing Commander Cheshire would be flying on ahead to illuminate the factory with red 'target indicators'.

As we approached the area, we could see a very faint red glow below us and we discussed the possibility of this being a German decoy. (It was a common enemy ploy to light dummy target indicators on open ground in the hope that we would waste our bombs there.)

Suddenly W/C Cheshire's voice came through on the R/T – "Sorry chaps, that one went through the roof, I'll try another one."

It transpired that Cheshire had dive-bombed the factory building with such accuracy that the target indicator had penetrated the factory roof and was burning on the floor inside the building, which explained why we could only see a faint glow through the hole in the roof.

Cheshire obligingly dropped a second red spot fire a few feet from the side of the building and we were easily able to aim our high explosive bombs with great precision. We were pleased to see photographs taken the next day showing the factory in ruins.

Although we were aware of the odds against our surviving for the mandatory thirty operations to complete one 'tour', we clung to the belief that 'it would'nt happen to us' and I used to think of Cheshire who had completed well over this number of operations.

On yet another Berlin operation we felt a loud 'clunk' from an exploding anti-aircraft shell while over the target, but as everything still appeared to be functioning normally, we dismissed the matter in our concentration to aim our bombs accurately.

It was only later that we noticed that the port inner engine was overheating badly and we were forced to reduce the throttle setting. When we did so, the temperature gauge would return to near normal, but we had to nurse the engine for the remainder of the long journey home. As usual, our faithful ground crew were waiting up to welcome us back, although they were officially 'off duty'and should have long since been in bed.

Slightly irritably, I said, "The port inner engine is on the blink," and strode off to the debriefing room. It was not until next morning that I discovered that the ground crew, despite being off duty, had insisted on carrying out an immediate inspection and found that a large area of the engine sump was missing, having been shot away when we heard that 'clunk'. A significant amount of engine oil had been lost and it was quite remarkable that the engine had continued to function for nearly four hours after such damage had occurred. Although the extreme cold conditions had helped to prevent the engine from seizing up, it is still a great tribute to Rolls-Royce, the makers of this famous 'Merlin' engine.

On 10th April 1944, our operation was to Tours and we were briefed to fly at only 5,500 ft, far lower than our operations over Germany. Instead of the customary heavy anti-aircraft fire, we were fascinated to watch the tracer bullets that seemed to be snaking lazily up towards us, giving us adequate time to alter course when necessary to avoid them. A French target such as this was a welcome relief from the far more hazardous operations over Germany.

During the next few days we carried out two more operations to Paris when once again the opposition was more of a token nature and there was no sign of enemy fighters, which were a much greater threat than gunfire from the ground.

Referring once again to our attack on the Junkers 88 factory at Toulouse, it was not until after the war that I became aware of just how great a menace this highly effective fighter/bomber had become, with its angled 20mm cannons mounted in the roof. The following page gives details. Once a German pilot had positioned his aircraft correctly below one of our bombers, their success rate in destroying the bomber was almost 100%. Unfortunately, we were unaware of this new technique at the time or we would most certainly have been more vigilant in watching directly beneath our aircraft, although there was a 'blind spot' below the Lancaster at which point the enemy could not be seen.

There were two occasions when thick fog on the return from operations necessitated us being diverted to an airfield elsewhere. The first time was on our return in a Wellington bomber from dropping leaflets over Paris when we landed at Tangmere in Sussex. A Canadian Spitfire Squadron was stationed there and it was the first that the pilots had seen of a Wellington at close range. It seemed enormous to them compared to the Spitfire.

The second time that we were diverted was after the successful bombing of the Junkers 88 factory and we were ordered to proceed to Wellesbourne. The weather was still unfit for us to return to base next morning so the seven of us took a trip into a nearby town. The only clothes that we had with us were our flying overalls and some of the locals seemed slightly bemused, at first believing that we might be shot down German aircrew. However, once our true identity had been established, it was "drinks all round".

The formidable Junkers 88R had two 20mm cannons mounted in the roof to fire diagonally upwards and slightly forwards. Having positioned himself below the bomber at a blind spot where he could not be seen, the pilot had ample time to aim upwards, being careful to avoid the bomb-bay, as the ensuing explosion would almost certainly have resulted in the destruction of not only the bomber, but the Junkers 88 too.

The technique was to fire at one of the two main fuel tanks in the wings; once the fuel ignited, the bomber would be doomed.

The new weapon was code named 'Schrage Musik', a literal translation being 'Slating Music' or 'Jazz Music'. Who said the Germans had no sense of humour?

In common with other returning aircrews, we had often reported seeing Lancaster or Halifax bombers suddenly exploding without warning, but had been informed that these were what became to be known as "Flaming Scarecrows" or harmless pyrotechnics fired up in an attempt to demoralise us.

Although some may have been of this nature, some that we saw from only a short distance away were definitely genuine bombers on fire.

Had we been briefed as to this new danger from the Junkers 88, we would certainly have been more vigilant in watching immediately below our aircraft.

On the night of 30/31st March 1944, in the course of an attack on Nuremberg, Bomber Command suffered its heaviest losses of the war. Due to a full moon, the dark painted bombers were silhouetted against the bright sky and the waiting enemy fighters could hardly fail to see and intercept them.

Of a total of 795 bombers, 95 failed to return, 12 more were lost after reaching England and a further 59 damaged. The total destroyed amounted to 13.5% with the loss of some 750 aircrew.

We were fortunate to be on a few days leave at that time, but on our return to the Squadron, so many familiar faces were missing that I was promoted to Acting Flight

Junkers JU88

Lieutenant, only six months after receiving my commission. In peacetime it would normally take two years to reach this rank.

As we had to maintain radio silence while over enemy territory to prevent our position from being plotted, one might wonder at the need for a wireless operator, but his duties were of vital importance.

Quite apart from assisting our Navigator by taking bearings on known radio transmissions as a check on our position, Jim, who had a nominal knowledge of German, spent his time listening for radio transmissions to and from enemy fighters and their ground control. We had a microphone located near one of the engines, and as soon as Jim heard any such transmissions, he merely had to flick a switch to send a deafening sound to blot out all attempts to communicate. He would stop for a second or two to listen to the angry frustrated voices before resuming.

The Germans were not slow to take measures in changing the radio frequency of their transmissions so that Jim needed to continually search the wavebands.

Jim was also responsible for operating our onboard radar, which was intended to give warning of the approach of enemy fighters but in practice their appearance was usually too sudden for it to be of much help.

CHAPTER 7

Our Luck Runs Out

On 22nd April 1944, our target was 'Brunswick' (spelt on some German maps as Braunschweig). For reasons that I could not define, an intense feeling of foreboding refused to go away. I felt compelled to write letters to my parents and my girlfriend telling them not to worry, as I somehow felt that I would survive. I wrote a further letter to the Station Adjutant requesting that he made arrangements for my car to be taken care of. I also asked one of my ground crew to look after my little dog, Boris. I had not felt the need to do any of these things prior to other operations.

It is true that we were to carry a 'second dickie' or second pilot on this occasion, a Flying Officer newly posted to the Squadron, and there was a superstition that this was unlucky, but I do not believe that this accounted for my presentiment of doom.

Incidentally, Boris was our crew mascot, so ugly that we named him after Boris Karloff whom we had seen in a

'Boris' on the tailplane of a Lancaster.

horror movie. Although strictly against regulations, Boris came with us on air-tests occasionally, although never on operations.

At briefing, we were given a short talk by the Chief Armaments Officer who told us that for the first time we were to carry the new "J" Type huge incendiary bombs.

"Once ignited", he said, "nothing known to man or beast can extinguish them." He added that the heat would be so intense that it would melt many metals. I was shortly to have verification of this.

My thoughts went back to the comparatively puny German incendiaries that I had partially extinguished with buckets of sand back in 1940. Because of the very high temperature of these new incendiaries, we were told that no fire-fighters would be able to get anywhere near them and that the idea of extinguishing one with a bucket of sand was ludicrous.

Quite often, operations would be cancelled due to deteriorating weather or other reasons, and I had always hated this after all the preparation, especially on the part of our Navigator. On this occasion, however, I was praying for a cancellation; but it was not to be.

Just before we boarded our Lancaster, a strange chance event was to make the difference between life and death for me.

Two types of parachute were available; the seat-type, which was securely strapped to the wearer and was usually favoured by pilots; and the clip-on chest-type worn by other crew members so as to give them greater mobility. In the case of our gunners there was little choice due to the confined space in the gun turret.

On joining the Squadron in August 1943, I had been issued with the usual seat-type parachute and had scrawled my name on as proof of ownership but shortly afterwards my parachute was either mislaid or taken by another pilot.

As no other seat-type parachute was available, I was issued with a clip-on chest-type, which I had used on every subsequent operation.

I had never been entirely happy with this arrangement as I felt that in an emergency, by the time I had held the aircraft steady for the remainder of the crew to bale out, there would be little opportunity for me to clip on my 'chute and escape also.

On calling at the parachute section prior to take off for this particular mission, much to my surprise, my original seat-type parachute was lying there with my name still scrawled on it. I did not establish where it had been for the past six months or who had been using it, but I greeted it like an old friend. In a few hours it was to save my life.

Due to the concentration needed whilst taking off, my feeling of impending doom was temporarily forgotten and it was not until later that I would recall it.

As was standard practice, we not only kept a sharp lookout for enemy fighters, but also watched the ground for flashes from anti-aircraft fire, but our progress so far was unopposed.

A FEW STATISTICS

LANCASTER
Four 1,460 hp Rolls Royce Merlin engines armed with four Browning .303 machine guns in the tail, two in the nose and two more in dorsal (mid upper) position. Top speed 275mph, but economical cruising speed only about 180mph.

MESSERSCHMITT 109
Three 20mm cannon plus Two 13mm machine guns. Top speed 386 mph.

JUNKERS JU88
Four 20mm cannon and two 13mm machine guns, plus the near vertical cannon on some versions referred to elswhere. Top speed 408 mph.

DeHAVILLAND MOSQUITO
Two Merlin 1,290hp engines. Top speed 341 mph. Unarmed.

At this stage of the war, the German air defences were in many ways superior to our own, or so it seemed to us. Certainly the almost invisible ultraviolet 'master' searchlights were highly efficient, as was the coordination between the fighters and their ground control. With such regular operations by the RAF and more recently the US Air Force, the defences were having plenty of opportunities to perfect their skills.

It was not until we approached the outer defences of Hanover to our right that, without any warning, there was a tremendous thud and within seconds flames appeared coming up through the floor at my feet. Even the metal alloy floor seemed to be on fire and I instinctively raised my feet from the rudder pedal and away from the floor as the flames started to engulf the front of the aircraft where I was sitting.

For a brief second I thought of the 'J-Type' incendiaries that we were carrying for the first time, and remembered that once ignited, nothing could extinguish them.

I raised my hand to switch on my microphone and give the order to "bale out", but before I could do so, the Lancaster exploded...

I can still recall shooting up through the shattered Perspex roof as everything disintegrated around me. There was a terrific jerk as my oxygen tube and intercom sockets were wrenched from their sockets, and one of my leather gauntlets was sucked from my hand. The violent change in velocity and oxygen deprivation caused me to almost black out for a short time, but I soon became partially conscious and was amazed to find that I was not only still alive, but appeared to be uninjured.

For some time, still in a daze, I watched the searchlight fingers from the Hanover area probing the sky, being quite unaware of the fact that I was rushing downwards at about 120mph.

It was not until I had dropped to a less rarified atmosphere with more oxygen that my wits returned with the sudden realisation that one vital action was needed if I was to stay alive for much longer. I reached across and pulled the ripcord of my parachute. The sudden tug as the canopy opened gave the impression of being dragged upwards. Seconds later I hit the ground quite heavily and was dragged over backwards by the still attached parachute. I had regained full consciousness just in time.

Apart from a pain in my back, I was still unhurt and released my parachute harness, later hiding the evidence as best I could in undergrowth. On clearing my ears, I could soon hear the sound of the bombers returning to their traditional bacon and egg late supper back home. I suddenly felt very lonely and sad at the thought of my

My final logbook entry of World War 2.
I have been marked down as 'missing'.

R.A.F. Skellingthorpe

YEAR 1944		AIRCRAFT		PILOT, OR 1ST PILOT	2ND PILOT, PUPIL OR PASSENGER	DUTY (INCLUDING RESULTS AND REMARKS
MONTH	DATE	Type	No.			
	—	:+ —	—	—	—	—— TOTALS BROUGHT FORWAR
RIL	5	LANCASTER III	LM476	SELF	CREW	Cancelled JU 88 FACTORY
	5		LM476	SELF	CREW	OPS. TOOLOUSE 12,500 ft.
	6		LM476	SELF	CREW	Wellesbourne to Base
	7		LM476	SELF	CREW F/O Pullman	TO SWINDERBY. AIR & SEA F
	8		LM476	SELF	CREW F/L Bean	H.L.B.
	8		LM476	SELF	CREW W/C St Dolph	Special Exercise
	10		LM476	SELF	CREW	Air test
	10		LM476	SELF	CREW	OPS. TOURS. 5,500 feet. B.L. 15,250 lbs.
	11		LM476	SELF	CREW	OPS. AACHEN 18,000ft.
	12		LM476	SELF	CREW	Bombing. Air Test
	16		(L)	SELF	CREW	TO SKELLINGTHORPE B.L. 14,000 lbs.
	18		LM476	SELF	CREW	OPS. PARIS AREA. 8,500 ft
	19		LM476	SELF	CREW	TO CRANWELL & RETURN
	20		LM476	SELF	CREW.	N.F.T.
	20.		LM476	SELF	CREW	OPS. PARIS.
	22		LM476	SELF	CREW	NFT Bombing.
	22		LM476	SELF	CREW	OPS. BRUNSWICK.
						MISSING

Summary for *April* , 19 44
Unit 61 Sqdn
Date 1/5/44
Signature *F. Mervin P/o*

1. Lanc III
2. ....
3. ....
4. ....

F. Smith F/L
OC A FLT.

S. Bankbeay W/C
OC. 61 Sq

GRAND TOTAL [Cols. (1) to (10)]
1630 Hrs. 55 Mins.

TOTALS CARRIED FORWA

crew, who I knew could not possibly have had time to clip on their chest-type parachutes to escape. Their parachutes were kept fixed to the side of the fuselage and it would have taken precious seconds to retrieve them, clip them on, and then bale out.

I knew that I was some distance west of Brunswick, and not too far from Hanover, and although not able to be more precise than that, I knew that it would be impossible to walk as far as the Dutch border many miles away. For aircrew baling out over the occupied countries there was always the chance, however slim, of getting in touch with the Resistance Movement, with whose help escape was possible, but in Germany no such help was forthcoming. Just as feelings ran high in Britain because of the Luftwaffe bombing, Germans who had suffered as a result of RAF and USAF attacks were certainly in no mood to offer assistance and were more likely to take matters into their own hands. Allied aircrew coming down over Germany were therefore very much on their own.

As it transpired, the Germans found the remains of our Lancaster next morning, together with the bodies of a pilot and six crew members. They had no reason to suspect that there were two pilots on this occasion and this was probably to my advantage in that they were not actively looking for anyone else, no other bomber having come down in the immediate vicinity.

Despite this small advantage, which did enable me to travel a few miles in a westerly direction, I knew it was only a matter of time before I would be too weak from lack of food to continue.

The escape kit which I always carried contained a map and small compass in addition to some Horlicks tablets and chocolate, etc, but no real food. It also contained a rubber water bottle with tablets to disinfect any stagnant water which I might find.

Despite having walked for quite some distance, I had needed to make numerous detours to avoid populated areas so had not gone very far in the westerly direction which I had planned.

I had been briefed in the event of being shot down to remove my pilot's brevet, DFC ribbon and rank braid so that I was left with a plain uniform, The tops of my flying boots were designed to be ripped off leaving serviceable walking shoes.

For a while I was in open country, but as dawn approached, I found a wooded area where I was glad to rest, remaining there for much of the day, only venturing on again as it started to get dark.

I avoided main roads, hoping to find a quite footpath leading in the right direction.

Eventually, weak from lack of food, and with a suspicious growth of beard, I was accosted by a member of the Hitler Youth who saw me before I had time to hide.

His opening words were, "Are you Englander?" to which I replied, "Nein", this being one of the very few German words of which I was capable. He hesitated for a moment and I continued to walk away only to be accosted for the second time with "Are you Englander?" Although the boy's English seemed rather limited, it was infinitely superior to my knowledge of German.

Two Wehrmacht soldiers joined the boy and pointed their Luger pistols at me, one grabing into my battledress pocket and pulling out my escape map.

Up to this moment they had been uncertain as to my identity as some foreign workers wore British battle-dress captured at Dunkirk in 1940, although these were more likely to be of a khaki colour.

Joined by a Wehrmacht officer, I was marched off to a nearby farmhouse where the farmer's wife kindly responded to my request for "wasser". Although I could have continued for some time without food, I was rapidly becoming dehydrated through lack of water and could not have gone on much longer without any.

I had a mutually non-productive interview with the local Gestapo official, who spoke no English, and after shouting at me for some time, he eventually gave up and I was escorted to the local jail at nearby Linden.

CHAPTER 8

Interrogation

My cell was only about 6ft by 4ft just large enough for a wooden bunk, but with no mattress, pillow or blankets, yet somehow I slept. Early next morning two Luftwaffe airmen arrived to escort me on the journey to Dulagluft, the main centre for the interrogation of captured allied airmen at Frankfurt-am-Main.

They spoke no English but pointed meaningfully to their Luger pistols, making it clear that they would shoot if I attempted to escape.

In a work of fiction, no doubt the captured airman would somehow overpower his armed guards and make a dramatic escape. However, this is a factual account, and I did neither of these.

During the long train journey I was able to witness the mile after mile of utter devastation caused by the bombing, yet where a factory chimney still stood, smoke could be seen coming from it, indicating that some production was still in progress. I had to admire their tenacity.

Due to the damage to the railways system, we had to change trains on several occasions. While we waited at the platform, civilians spat at me, calling me "Terrorbomber" or "Luftgangster". I was glad of the protection provided by my escort.

Soon after arrival at Dulagluft, I was marched before a Luftwaffe Major who spoke perfect English without a trace of a foreign accent. I gave him my name, rank and service number. He had in front of him my pilot's brevet, rank braid and DFC ribbon, which had been found in my battledress pocket when I was captured.

I was returned to my cell, only to be brought back to the Major next morning, when he enquired, "Where have you been hiding for the past six months?"

At the time I was quite unaware of the reason for this question, but it was obvious that he was not satisfied with my answers.

Whereas other captured airmen seemed to have just one short interrogation before being sent to a prisoner of war camp, I was destined to remain at Dulagluft for longer.

At the third interview, the Major said, "I regret that I have no alternative but to refer this matter to higher authority". I did not like the inference of this remark as I had visions of the Gestapo's methods of interrogation.

I was more than relieved the next day when the Major greeted me with a wide smile. "You could have saved us both so much trouble if you had told me the facts," he said while passing over to me a copy of *The London Gazette* Supplement with the details of my award of the DFC.

Evidently, by an incredible coincidence, I had been captured in almost the same spot that my three former crew members had been found six months previously. This fact, plus the claim by the Luftwaffe fighter pilots that our aircraft had definitely been shot down on the earlier occasion, had caused the confusion.

I do not really believe that the German authorities thought I had been wandering around Germany for six months without being apprehended, but they had to make sure. Perhaps they were concerned in case a traitor had given me shelter, but this is only conjecture on my part.

The Germans, with their usual efficient cross-filing system, being in possession of my name, rank and number, and knowing that I had a DFC, merely had to look through copies of the *London Gazette Supplement* to find the edition listing details of my award. This not only gave them my name and number, but also my squadron number, which I had not revealed!

The major seemed genuinely please to have resolved the matter without the need for "higher authority", as was I, and for a time we almost forget that we were on opposite sides in a war. He saw from his records that after the capture of my three former crew members, a fruitless search was made for me and the three remaining crew. How the German authorities discovered my name as the pilot, I did not establish.

It had come through some weeks previously, via the International Red Cross that Sergeant Cronchie, the mid-upper gunner, had died from his wounds after capture, but the Navigator and Bomb-aimer were both prisoners of war.

The Major now suggested, "We Germans and you British should settle our differences and fight together against the common foe". When I enquired who he was referring to as "the common foe", he replied, "The Bolsheviks".

"But they are on *our* side," I replied, and at this he gave up. However, during the cold war period I often recalled his words.

Now that he was in such a friendly mood, I asked how Germany hoped to win the war with not only Britain and the British Empire to fight (we still had an Empire then), but also Russia and The United States. The Major merely shrugged, but I believe he knew in his heart the futility of it all.

Next, still under escort, I undertook the long journey to Stalag Luft 3 POW Camp in Poland, where it had just been announced that fifty British and Allied prisoners had been shot following a mass escape attempt the previous month.

This tragic event has been well documented and was made into the film *The Great Escape*, starring Steve McQueen, Richard Attenborough, James Garner and many others. After the war, all surviving inmates of Stalag Luft 3 were invited to the premiere of the film at the Odeon Cinema in Leicester Square.

Evidently the Germans planted English-speaking spies into the camp, posing as captured RAF Officers, and for this reason all new arrivals were vetted to establish their true identity. A Canadian pilot from my Squadron, shot down a few weeks previously, was able to vouch for me, and we soon became close friends. I always knew him as 'Johnny' Johnson and it never occurred to me to enquire if he was actually christened John.

We spent many hours during the following months walking around the perimeter circuit discussing hair-brained plans of escape. Johnny was keen for us to climb the barbed-wire, make our way to a Luftwaffe airfield and commandeer an aircraft and fly home. We both knew that all escape attempts had to be sanctioned by the Escape Committee and that this mad idea would be rejected out of hand, but just discussing it gave us something to do.

I had only been at the camp for a few weeks when, on the 6th June, 1944, we heard of the Allied invasion. We had a secret radio receiver and were able to listen to the BBC Overseas News bulletins daily.

The German radio briefly mentioned the landing and claimed that "the last Allied soldier will have been eliminated by midnight." Next day, however, they admitted that "Mopping-up operations were still in progress". Each day the German radio claimed to have repulsed the enemy with heavy losses, but the place names mentioned indicated how the Allies were advancing.

Before continuing with further events, I must go back to some experiences at Stalag Luft 3, one of which was to involve another 'against all the odds' situation some twenty years later.

When I first arrived, British prisoners were in a separate compound from the Americans, but as the months went by and a growing number of US officers were captured, the American compound became too small to hold any more, and new US arrivals were moved into the British camp.

The room which I shared with five other RAF officers had an additional two-level bunk added so as to accommodate two US officers, a B17 pilot and a Bombardier (the American name for Bomb-aimer).

We quickly became friendly with our new arrivals, calling them "Colonials" and they in turn calling us "Limeys" – but only in fun.

The US pilot had a distinctive accent which reminded me of the voice of James Stewart, the Hollywood star, who was also a pilot during the war. This was to have a sequel many years later as mentioned above.

Whereas RAF officers from shot down Lancasters, Halifaxes or other aircraft usually arrived singly or no more than two from any one aircraft, US officers frequently arrived in groups of as many as ten at a time.

On night-time operations, RAF aircrews did everything possible to stay with their aircraft, even though it was damaged, in the hope of being able to make it back, but daytime tactics of the USAF were quite different.

The Americans explained that the German fighters would single out an unfortunate B17 or B34 (Liberator to us) and attack it from all sides. Usually three or four fighters would keep attacking until the gunners in the bomber ran out of ammunition – a real 'war of attrition'.

At this stage the bomber was defenceless, with no hope of reaching its base during daylight hours.

The US bombers flew in close formation for mutual fire support and once a bomber fell out of formation, its destruction by fighters was almost certain. In such a situation, the crew of the stricken aircraft would be forced to bale out – assuming they were still alive and able to do so – and this accounted for the somewhat larger numbers of US officers arriving at the camp.

Formation flying at night was, needless to add, quite impracticable without navigation lights, and was therefore never attempted.

Making conversation with our US Bombardier, I mentioned that I had trained in Canada, and was rather amazed when he enquired, "Do they have pound notes in Canada, the same as in England?" As the US has a 3,000 mile border with Canada, I had assumed that he would know of the Canadian dollar, but he came from one of the Southern States, many miles from the Canadian border and this was 1943. Nowadays, with foreign holidays being so commonplace, I am sure that most Americans would be better informed on such matters.

I have no way of verifying the truth of the following two items but have no reason to doubt their authenticity.

One officer, previously of Coastal Command and flying an obsolete 'Walrus' flying-boat, claimed to have been shot down before he knew that we were at war! According to his story, he was on a patrol over the Atlantic Ocean when he spotted a submarine emerge and decide to "shoot it up" for a bit of fun. I gather that Britain had declared war on Germany some minutes earlier, but this information had not reached this unfortunate pilot who was promptly shot down by the submarine – a German U-Boat. When he was hauled out of the sea and informed, as was customary, "For you the war is over," in surprise he had asked, "What war?"

Another officer, shot down during the opening weeks of the war, claimed to have been treated to a meal by Herman Goering, Chief Air Marshal of the Luftwaffe. According to his story, Goering told him not to worry as the war would be over in a couple of weeks and he would then be able to go home.

As the weeks turned to months and then years, it must have been soul-destroying to have had nearly five years of his life wasted in a POW camp, but, all considered, he seemed reasonably cheerful.

At least when I was captured it was only a few weeks before we learned of the Allied invasion of Europe and we knew that we were starting to win the war.

We had a large map of Germany on the community room wall at Stalag Luft 3 with drawing pins and coloured tape to represent both the Western and Eastern fronts. Although we knew from listening to BBC Overseas transmissions on our clandestine radio that a certain town or district was in Allied hands, we had to wait until this was admitted on the German news bulletins before we could alter our map. Each week the two fronts moved closer together and the German Camp Commandant would come to look at our map shaking his head and muttering "All is *kaput!*" It was fortunate for him that no Gestapo officials could hear him, or he would probably have been shot for defeatism.

We POWs were becoming progressively weaker, because the Red Cross parcels were now reduced to one parcel between two men each week, the German authorities considering their delivery to be of low priority. Although we were reduced to remaining in bed to conserve our strength, the guards still insisted on counting us twice daily to make sure that no escapes had taken place.

Some enterprising prisoners initiated an organisation known as 'Foodacco', where food could be exchanged for cigarettes and vice-versa. Every item in the Red Cross parcels was given a points value. The prisoners running the service charged a small points commission on each transaction, and like the Stock Exchange, the points value of any item would vary according to supply and demand.

Over the months, some shrewd operators had accumulated an amazing number of points and were known as "Foodacco Millionaires". Unfortunately all these points became worthless when the order came to evacuate the camp. Perhaps after the war some of them made a real fortune on the real stock market.

Despite our meagre food rations, some prisoners still traded in some of their food in exchange for cigarettes and I was glad not to have become addicted to smoking.

One other episode is worth recording if only for its rarity, and this concerns the Russian prisoners at the camp, who really were almost starving. Because Russia was not a member of the International Red Cross, they did not received any food parcels and had to rely on what little the Germans gave them.

They would enter our compound regularly to clean out the toilets and carry out other menial tasks, always accompanied by a German guard, and it was impossible for us to communicate with them in any way during this time. On other occasions however, we often saw them the other side of the barbed wire engaged in some form of manual labour, and it was then that we would attempt to throw them scraps of food.

We had to be certain that no guards were watching, as it was strictly against the regulations for us to do this. One particular Russian would always smile and acknowledge any items of food that we were able to throw over the wire. We did not expect anything back in return as the Russian prisoners had virtually no personal possessions of any kind.

Much to my surprise therefore, this same Russian, having made certain that no guards were watching, threw something over for me to pick up. It was a hand-made cigarette case which he had fashioned out of an old piece of scrap sheet metal. It was decorated on each side with an intricate pattern, and by sign language he gestured with a nail and a large stone to demonstrate how he had made the pattern using the stone as a hammer and the nail to form the design.

Long before I came to be an inmate of the camp serious problems had occurred in trying to dig escape tunnels due to the nature of the soft sandy soil which tended to cause any tunnel to collapse. It must have been quite traumatic for anyone digging to have the tunnel collapse behind him thus trapping him until the blockage could be cleared.

Each sleeping bunk was supplied with seven wooden slats, each the width of the bunk to support a straw mattress or palliasse. It was soon found that these boards were ideal for supporting the sides and roof of any tunnel to prevent it from collapsing.

As the Escape Committee had first priority on any items that could be useful in an escape attempt, they soon started to requisition as many of these boards as might be required for this purpose.

When the first of these tunnels was discovered by the Germans, orders were given to the security guards, known to us as "ferrets", to regularly inspect our bunks to make sure that the regulation number of seven boards per bed were present.

Someone had the idea of splitting the boards width-ways in half so as to preserve the correct number, although obviously the slats were narrower than before This tended to make sleeping rather uncomfortable as the straw palliasse would sag in the gaps between the boards.

Incredibly, the ferrets had only been instructed to count that there were seven boards per bunk, and not report on the obvious fact that the boards had suddenly become half of their previous width. We found such lack of initiative on the guards' part to be incredible but they were only trained to carry our orders to the letter and no more and thus we were able to provide the timber needed for future tunnel escapes.

By December 1944, the Russians, who had been advancing westwards for much of the year, were close to the bank of the River Oder, the border between occupied Poland and Germany.

Once the Russians crossed the river, they would be on German soil for the first time, and Hitler issued an order to his Panzer Troops "not to budge another inch under any circumstances".

Although they had been retreating all the way from the gates of Stalingrad and were short of fuel and ammunition, as well as suffering from frostbite, the German troops were so terrified of Hitler's wrath that they made a last stand and held up the Russian advance for a few days.

It was in that few days that the Germans made the decision to evacuate our camp and move us west, away from the dreaded Russian advance. It was also then that we received our last mail from home.

There were three items of mail for me. One was a letter from Ruth, the young lady with whom I had become acquainted while I had been in Canada and who wrote faithfully to me every week during my stay in POW camp. Captured Germans sent to Canada enjoyed a relaxed existence with ample food, very different from our life in a German POW camp. This fact was recognised by the German authorities and letters from Canada were given some form of priority compared to incoming mail from elsewhere.

My second letter was from my parents to tell me that all was well and that my car had arrived safely home from the squadron and was being cared for by them.

The third item was a postcard which merely had the following words written on it:

Having a lovely time. Wish you were here.

It was signed 'Lucky Davis'.

I had to read it twice before comprehension sunk in. By some sort of miracle, my Navigator was not only alive and well but back in England!

In view of the traumatic and almost instantaneous disintegration of our Lancaster and the fact that none of the crew could possibly have had time to clip on their chest-type parachutes, it really did seem unbelievable. Despite my immediate rather uncertain future, this postcard really made my day.

It was not until my return home after the war that I met up with Lucky and learned the full story of his extraordinary escape.

Just seconds before the explosion that destroyed our Lancaster, Lucky had a strong premonition, or perhaps a sixth sense, that prompted him to reach out into the fuselage and obtain his parachute. He had just clipped on one side only when he could remember being literally sucked out through a huge hole that appeared at his side as the aircraft disintegrated.

Although he had no recollection of pulling the rip-cord of his parachute as was barely conscious, he must have done so as it was not designed to open without this vital action.

The Germans found him next morning lying on the side of a hill with a broken neck, but still alive. They confirmed that only one side of his parachute was attached.

He was taken to a military hospital where his neck and upper torso were encased in a plaster cast which remained on for some months. As his injuries precluded him from returning to active service, it was arranged via The Red cross for him to be returned to England in exchange for a badly injured Luftwaffe crew man.

Despite his injuries, Lucky lived up to his nickname by once again surviving against all the odds.

As soon as it was announced that we were to vacate the camp in 24 hours time, there was furious activity in the various barrack blocks as prisoners tried to improvise makeshift backpacks to hold as many food rations as possible.

The Germans were unlikely to supply much, if any, food on the journey and it was considered essential to take as much as was humanly possible.

Johnny Johnson and I made our plans to hide behind in the expectation of being liberated by the advancing Russian troops

That night we managed to climb out of a window of our barrack building without being seen. The Germans had boarded up the doors at each end to prevent anyone from leaving.

Our block – number 20 – was nearest to the camp theatre, a similar wooden structure, and under cover of darkness, we were able to reach it without much trouble.

All the barrack blocks, including the theatre building, were raised 12 to 18 inches above ground level, supported by timber blocks, to prevent damp penetration, and we were able to crawl under where we spent a most uncomfortable night in the freezing conditions.

The Germans had been told that if they were caught by the Russians, they would be mercilessly tortured and then killed, thus their haste to depart as quickly as possible. In their confusion and near panic, we were able to remain undetected while the main party of prisoners marched away next morning.

Our freedom was short lived however as a rear-guard had been ordered to remain behind to round up any "strays" such as ourselves. We were soon spotted and marched away at gun-point..

We both put on exaggerated limps, and pointed to our legs, saying, "Kaput, kaput." We were taken to the camp sick quarters where it was found that all the medical staff had already left and there was no one qualified to examine us

We were given the benefit of the doubt and were destined to travel by cattle truck to an unknown destination further west and away from the dreaded Russians.

An old farm wagon was the only transport available to take us to the railway station at nearby Sagan. It was drawn by one horse and one ox, making an unwieldy pair, the horse trying to go faster than the slower but more powerful ox. It gave us an indication of the depths to which the once proud "Third Reich" had descended.

The rail wagons, taken over from the French, had a notice "40 hommes or 20 cheveaux". There were no horses, but well over the regulation 40 men were forced into each wagon. Try as we did to remain together, Johnny and I became separated and I never saw him again.

Where as the main body of prisoners on the march had taken with them as much food as they could carry, Johnny and I had made no contingency plans in the event of capture and had very little with us apart from some cigarettes.

I was now able to barter some food in exchange for cigarettes, the latter being far more portable than tins of food. I had not brought any drinking vessel with me and was reduced to using an old tin can to drink from.

The wagon was so crowded that we were crammed together, unable to either sit or lie down in any comfort, but worse was to come.

The RAF were bombing the railways every night and the Americans during the daytime, with bombs sometimes dropping all around us.

Our wagon was shunted into a siding while the guards took shelter as best they could. One very slim prisoner, by stripping to the waist, managed to squeeze out through one of the narrow ventilation gaps, although these were only about 9 or ten inches by 30 inches.

Moments later we heard firing and we assumed that the escapee had been shot. In retaliation the guards boarded up the ventilation gaps from the outside to prevent further escape attempts. With so many men in such a confined space and without any fresh air able to enter the wagon, the atmosphere soon became almost impossible to breathe due to lack of oxygen and we were close to suffocating.

I must have been quite ill because I can recall an American banging on the door and yelling, "Open up. We have a man dying in here". A guard slid back the door, took one look at me, and escorted me out to sit with him up front in the glorious fresh air.

I soon recovered, only to be ordered back into the fetid conditions inside. I cursed myself for not having had the sense to sham illness for a bit longer.

Each day the sliding doors were opened and a few of us at a time were permitted out to attend to the calls of nature. A bucket of water, contaminated by smuts from the engine, was passed to us daily and occasionally a container of watery potato soup, but no other food.

Although initially we considered ourselves fortunate to be travelling by train instead of the forced march of the main party, we soon felt that despite the bitter winter weather in Poland, anything would have been preferable to the seven days nightmare journey in that wagon.

Prisoners on the march later told me that their experiences had been equally grim in many ways. Prized possessions were soon discarded due to the owners' inability to carry them any longer. Makeshift backpacks had been made by sewing up the waist of old pairs of trousers and wrapping the trouser legs around.

After a few miles with tins of food digging them in the back, many prisoners were in extreme discomfort. The lucky ones found a barn or other shelter at night because to sleep out under such freezing conditions was to court frostbite.

One prisoner related to me how when he awoke one morning he found a guard had died during the night. He was frozen solid still clutching his rifle.

At least we had youth on our side, whereas most of the German guards were quite elderly.

Eventually we reached our destination, a derelict transit camp some where in East Germany, and the state of the accommodation was so bad that we elected to sleep out in the open for the first night. Next day was spent in cleaning out the filth and squalor left by the previous occupants until the place became reasonably habitable.

We soon found that the only way to survive was to join a small group, because anyone on their own was at a great disadvantage. A line-up of men waiting for drinking water would often coincide with another group waiting for soup and a single prisoner would have to decide which queue to join. Supplies frequently ran out before everyone had been served.

I still only had my tin as a drinking vessel and it was by now showing signs of rust, but I was no worse off than many others as everything was in such short supply.

By March of 1945, we were once again ordered to evacuate the camp as the Russian troops were fast approaching. This time, wooden leg or not, there was no alternative but to walk, no transport being available.

Fortunately, the weather was becoming milder and I quickly discovered that my remaining few cigarettes were almost worth their weight in gold. I was able to trade with local farmers as we passed through various villages; a standard rate of one cigarette for one egg soon becoming established.

It was interesting to watch how a battered packet of cigarettes changed hands time after time until the contents were practically unsmokeable, yet it would be accepted without question, having become an almost universal unofficial 'currency', barter of one kind or another having largely replaced the almost worthless official German paper money.

My only somewhat half-hearted attempt to escape was during March in the Spring sunshine. For quite a long time there was a thick forest of trees to our left and I noticed that the guard ahead rarely bothered to look back. The guards were spaced at intervals at the side of the marching column of men, and occasionally as we rounded a bend, I would be momentarily out of sight of the guard behind me. I was on the outside of the three-deep column and by timing things well, I was able to stumble into the thick undergrowth without being seen, the man in the centre quickly taking my place so that my absence was not noticed.

I have to confess that my action was motivated more by the strong need to rest than any real plan of escape. I was still wearing my flying boots, which had never been designed for long route marches, and I had started to develop blisters on both feet.

The long column of men seemed to continue endlessly past as I tried to crawl deeper into the forest without being seen, and soon I fell asleep from sheer exhaustion.

I have no idea how long I rested, but I was awakened by two elderly men from the German equivalent of our Home Guard who had been detailed to search the woods for any escapees.

I was escorted at gunpoint back to the road, where still more prisoners were passing. After a few words with the guards, I was orderd back into the column where they now kept me in sight more diligently.

Compared to those fifty prisoners from Stalag Luft 3 who were shot for doing their duty in attempting to escape, I was fortunate in not suffering any form of punishment.

By the middle of March, we arrived at our final POW camp, by which time the Germans had nowhere left to take us due to the rapid advances of the British and Americans from the West and the Russians from the East.

Despite our acute shortage of food, some prisoners were still willing to exchange what little food they had for cigarettes. As one of them explained to me, "Smoking stops me feeling hungry". This was rather a vicious circle, as the less food that he had, the more was his craving to smoke to relieve his hunger pangs.

Despite these conditions, most prisoners survived remarkably well, being young and relatively fit. It is surprising how little food is required to stay alive, at least in the short-term.

One prisoner, however, I did feel sorry for. He had been diagnosed as suffering from a duodenal ulcer and was forbidden to either smoke or eat almost all of the limited range of food that was available. Fortunately his period of incarceration would soon be at an end.

After the more orderly life at Stalag Luft 3 when we had our secret radio receiver and heard the BBC overseas news bulletins each day, we were now almost completely out of touch with the latest events and craved for any information we could glean.

Excitement was mounting when we witnessed some US Thunderbolt fighter aircraft strafing the ground quite close to us with cannon fire. Suddenly we saw an airman descending by parachute to land in the middle of our makeshift camp.

It was the pilot of one of the fighters, and as we gathered around him someone said, "You sure have landed in the right place!" All of us, including this airman, had a good laugh and we were more than delighted to learn that the Allied authorities were aware of the position of our camp and all personnel had been briefed not to bomb or strafe it.

This American was shot down on 21st April 1945. The very next day the US Third Army reached our camp, so he must hold some sort of record for the shortest period of captivity for any POW!

Only seconds before the first US Sherman tank lumbered into the camp, the German guards had their machine guns trained on us and we wondered if we were to be shot, but as the huge tank came into view, the guards climbed down from their gun-posts and we could see some donning civilian clothes.

Acknowledging our cheers of welcome, the first tank driver looked around and asked, "What are you guys still doing in here?". We told him that moments before we had been covered by machine guns from the guards, but as there was not a German to be seen now, he found it difficult to believe us.

When they saw the formidable Sherman tanks coming in their direction, the Germans were very good at becoming invisible and melting into the background. As the guards had only been armed with light machine guns, useless against the heavily armoured tanks, they could hardly be blamed.

Fresh excitement arose as General George Patton strode into the camp. He really was a larger than life character with two 'six shooters' stuck in his belt.

He made a short speech in which he, said, "You men have conducted your selves admirably under adverse circumstances", and then he was gone, as suddenly as he had arrived, to continue chasing the Germans.

As a last gesture of defiance, we raided the German records office and I was able to retrieve the record card that held my personal details.

My POW record card and identitiy card, liberated from the offices at Stalag Luft III after our liberation by the US 3rd Army under General Patton.

CHAPTER NINE

The First Post War 'Tourists'

My new found friend, a Major in the US Air Force, gave me his nearly new leather flying jacket in exchange for my RAF battledress blouse, and although I felt that I had the best of the bargain, I understood his wish to have something different to wear. That leather jacket was in regular use by me for many years.

This final stage of our forced stay in Germany was strange, in that General Patton and the US combat troops had left our vicinity to continue chasing the Germans, but the military government had not yet arrived. I only knew the Major as "Hank, and in deciding to venture forth into the village, we were about to embark upon what was in some ways, perhaps the most bizarre event of all.

We found an old barn, and inside was an equally ancient car which had been laid up for the war. It was covered in straw and the tyres were flat, but this did not deter Hank, who was quite sure that we would be able to get it going.

With some difficulty we pushed it out to the road while an elderly man watched us from behind a curtained window of the adjacent house, but made no attempt to interfere. German civilians were used to obeying anyone in uniform, and although we had no weapons of any kind, he probably did not know that.

On closer examination, we found that there was no fuel in the tank and the battery seemed to be dead, but Hank soon hailed a passing jeep laden with German helmets. The driver was more than pleased to take time off from fighting the war to assists us.

He produced a jerry can, filled up the 'gas' tank and then obligingly pumped up the tyres. Requesting that we sat in the old car to steer, he then shunted us from behind with his jeep, disdaining the use of a tow-rope.

With clouds of black smoke interspersed with a few bangs, we were shunted around the village square, until, with the car in gear, the engine reluctantly fired, unevenly at first, but more smoothly as it warmed up.

Knowing that we had been prisoners of war, the jeep driver gave us a carton of 200 'Lucky Strike' cigarettes, worth a small fortune on the black market, and then he went on his way.

As the battery was still flat, Hank suggested that we should go for a drive to charge it up, but we had only travelled a few miles before we were stopped by an incredulous US Military Policeman who looked in disbelief at our old car and said, "Don't you know there's a war on?" Then seeing Hank's rank of Major, he saluted and said, "Is there anything I can do for you, sir?"

Hank explained that we wished to drive on in order to charge up the battery, and the Sergeant considered this for a moment, and then said, "Perhaps I can help you sir". Asking us to wait for a minute, he soon returned with a US flag, which he attached to the windscreen. "This should prevent you from being stopped at every intersection" he said, and thanking him, we proceeded on our way, oblivious to the stares of soldiers and civilians alike.

In exchange for a few cigarettes, Hank purchased various items as souvenirs to take back home, as I enjoyed the Spring sunshine.

Eventually we were stopped again by a burly US Sergeant who began, "Where the hell do you think you're going?" but once again, seeing Hank's rank, said, "I think it would be better, sir, if you don't go on any further. We are having a little spot of bother up ahead."

We parked the car on the grass verge with the engine left running with instructions to the Sergeant to keep an eye on it. If we switched off the engine we were afraid it would not start again.

In deference to the Major's rank, we were permitted to proceed on foot, and we could soon see several tanks ahead arranged in a semi-circle firing at almost point-blank range at what appeared to be a warehouse of some kind.

At each explosion from the guns, the whole building seemed to shake and we could not believe that there could be anyone left alive inside, but suddenly the firing stopped and moments later two very shaken and grimy Hitler Youths staggered out, evidently not seriously wounded.

One boy defiantly gave the Nazi salute and was promptly knocked to the ground by one of the soldiers.

Incredibly, on interrogation, the two boys actually believed that they were still winning the war and that at any moment a German regiment would appear from 'around the corner' to rescue them. Such is the power of propaganda! In little more than a week the war would be over.

Shortly afterwards, returning to the car with Hank driving, we returned by a different route, stopping once or twice for Hank to look for any souvenirs although very little of any value was forthcoming.

Before long we met up with a US Army Captain and his platoon, and on hearing that we only had a POW camp to return to, he ordered his troops to remove at gun point the civilian occupants of a block of luxury flats and invited us to be his guests there.

The Germans had been evicted so suddenly that there were still cups of warm coffee on the table as we entered. For the first time since being captured we were able to enjoy the luxury of a hot bath.

We can truthfully claim to have been the first post war tourists in Europe – nearly ten days before the end of the war!

After two days, sadly, we had to leave our pampered existence to return to the camp so that the authorities would know where we were, and shortly afterwards Hank and the other Americans ex-prisoners were flown first to England and then home, but not before Hank, who had a conscience, had returned the car to its rightful owner.

It was to be an agonising ten days before the remainder of us were back in England, by which time VE Day (Victory Europe Day) had come and gone.

During this period, I was detailed by the senior British officer to arrange for guards to be placed on a store of Red Cross parcels which we found nearby, as he was concerned that it would be raided by the local civilian population, many of whom were near to starving. I organised a 'two hours on and four hours off' guard duty.

Many elderly civilians came begging for food, and all seemed to have the same story: "We were never Nazis, but what could we do?" Nobody admitted to having been a Nazi at that time.

One elderly man, who spoke quite good English, showed me a picture of his wife and told me that she had been arrested a year a ago because she had complained about some trivial matter. He had not seen or heard from her since and had no idea if she was alive or dead. Evidently a neighbour, who they thought was their friend, had reported his wife for "defeatist remarks".

Although I was generally hard-hearted when it came to requests for food from the Germans, I did relent on this occasion and passed over a tin of Spam.

Having been on near starvation rations for the past year, we now had food to spare because, apart from the store of Red Cross parcels, the US Third Army had been more than generous with various supplies.

One rather curious item that the Americans wheeled into our camp was a doughnut machine! A mixture of white flour, sugar and other ingredients were added, and then heated in the machine by means of propane gas or similar fuel. A handle was then cranked and out came the doughnuts, one at a time.

However, after the very dense German bread to which we had become accustomed, we all suffered from flatulence from them, although, as there was no instruction manual, perhaps we did not cook them correctly!

After the luxury of driving around in a vintage car, I refused to walk and apprehended a bicycle for the short journey from the camp to the Red Cross store and back.

Despite the surplus of food available, most of us found that we could only eat surprisingly small amounts, which was rather frustrating. After so long on such short rations, our digestive systems simply could not cope with large meals.

At last, after we had begun to wonder if we had been forgotten, a US Dakota transport aircraft arrived at a nearby landing strip, and whereas my companions marched to the airfield, I pedalled my bicycle there. I abandoned it a few yards from the Dakota only to see it retrieved by one of the aircraft crew who took it on board as a souvenir.

We were flown as far as Reims in France where some Lancasters were lined up for the final part of our journey home.

Ignoring our protests, well-meaning RAF Medical Staff insisted on spraying us very thoroughly with white de-lousing powder; down our trousers and necks and everywhere else. It was quite useless for me to try to tell them that I had been enjoying the luxury of hot baths only days before and was definitely not lousy.

On arriving back in England, we had to endure the whole process yet again – but we were so overjoyed at being home that we no longer cared.

All ex prisoners of war who had been in captivity for one year or more were given the opportunity for immediate release from the Services, and I actually just qualified. I had been shot down on 22nd April 1944 and was liberated by General Patton's US Third Army on 22nd April 1945.

Despite my experiences however, I had not lost my love of flying and requested to return to any form of flying that was available. Those of us who did not opt for immediate release could choose to be trained in any branch of the Service.

I arrived back in England on 11th May, 1945 and was granted generous leave until 2nd September – ample time to 'rehabilitate'.

I was delighted to discover that my little Singer sports car had arrived safely back and that my parents had gone to some expense in having a smart new black hood fitted to replace the old one which had been in a very poor state of repair.

On 3rd September I was posted to West Malling in Kent for a refresher course, and it was not long before ex-prisoners of the Japanese started to arrive back.

These ex-prisoners of the Japanese had such harrowing tales to tell of their hardships and the brutality of their captors that, by comparison, I felt that I had got off lightly. The peculiar situation with the Germans was that we could go over their country to bomb them yet if shot down and captured we were, by and large, treated correctly according to international conventions for the treatment of prisoners, very different to the attitude of the Japanese.

Political prisoners in Germany, especially anyone heard to criticise Hitler or the Nazi regime however, were treated extremely harshly, many ending up in concentration camps.

The one obvious exception to this general rule was the shooting of the fifty or so RAF officers following the mass breakout in march, 1944, referred to earlier in this book. The Luftwaffe officials would not have sanctioned any such action as they accepted that it was every prisoner's duty to attempt escape. They were also well aware that their own airmen had bombed London and many other cities, often indiscriminately.

After the war it became known that Hitler was so incensed to learn of the large number of RAF prisoners who had broken out of Stalag Luft 3 and the many thousands of troops involved in their recapture that he ordered everyone in involved in the escape to be shot.

It was only the intervention of Air Marshal Goering that prompted Hitler to amend the order. Goering pointed out that if all the prisoners were shot, he would be unwilling to order his Luftwaffe aircrew to bomb Britain for fear of reprisals if they were shot down. Hitler walked off in a rage saying, "Shoot fifty of them then", and this, sadly, is what took place. A Luftwaffe official had the grim task of deciding which officers should die and who should be spared.

As the theme of this book is "against all the odds", it seems appropriate to include a few such items.

Although I am unable to offer any logical reason why it should be so, "million to one" chance encounters do seem to occur more frequently that might be expected by mere chance.

What must be the odds against my capture taking place where three of my crew had baled out and been captured seven months previously on route to a quite different target?

What strange premonition urged Lucky Davis, our Navigator, to reach out for his parachute just seconds before the aircraft was hit and disintegrated? Up to that moment we had not seen a single enemy fighter in the sky and no anti-aircraft fire in our vicinity.

Some years after the war, my wife and I were on holiday in Morocco and having, like most tourists, done the rounds of the kasbah we entered the Cafe de Paris for cool drinks. We watched the world go by the window, fascinated by the many different faces from white to jet-black with every shade of brown in between. As we sipped our drinks, a voice from behind me enquired, "Pardon me, is this seat taken?" Without even looking round, I exclaimed, "I know that voice!" It was the B17 pilot with the distinctive voice with whom I had shared a room at Stalag Luft 3. The meeting was all the more remarkable because, like many American tourists, he and his wife were intent on visiting as many places as possible during their vacation and were only scheduled to be in Morocco for a few hours.

Inevitably we were more than interested to learn of each other's experiences after the camp was vacated. While our respective wives discussed the things that ladies everywhere like to talk about, we discussed flying and kindred matters.

Another "million to one" encounter involved a long standing friend, Seymour Jaffe, director of a drug company, and if one looks in any telephone directory, the name Jaffe is unlikely to occur very often.

Seymour arranged a meeting with a business contact, and as they had not previously met, it was agreed that they should rendezvous under the clock of a large London rail terminal. Seymour arrived a few minutes early and could see an individual also standing there, glancing in his direction. After a few moments, this person came over to Seymour and enquired, "Are you Dr Jaffe?"

Slightly taken aback, Seymour replied, "My name is Jaffe, but I am not a doctor". The man looked equally surprised and explained that he was due to meet a Dr Jaffe at precisely the same time and place as Seymour's rendezvous.

Shortly afterwards the real Dr Jaffe arrived, as did Seymour's contact and all was explained.

The odds against two individuals with such an unusual name arranging to quite independently two separate meetings at the same moment in time and at the same place must be astronomical!

Perhaps someone reading this book will be able to offer some explanation as to why such events occur.

Despite my experiences, I had not lost my love of flying, and signed on for a further two years, soon being posted to No. I Advanced Flying Unit, first at Wheaton Aston, and later at Moreton-in-Marsh. We helped to pioneer "blind" landings, purely on instruments and with the aid of radio signals. It was strange to approach the runway without being able to see out of the cockpit and actually touch down safely.

Some years later, after having resumed civilian life, I became a gliding instructor at weekends at RAF Kenley, a famous former Battle of Britain Spitfire base, where I helped teach Air Cadets to fly fairly basic glider aircraft and eventually to go solo in them.

Since retiring, I have managed a few flights as pilot on single-engined light aircraft at Goodwood, near Chichester, not far from my home.

Despite being searched by the Germans a number of times after being captured, my escape compass, deep in my battledress trouser pocket, was never discovered and I still have it to this day. It measures only a half inch across, yet, despite having suffered a cracked glass front, it still works perfectly. A tribute to British craftsmanship.

With their insistence on carrying out orders, even when they no longer served any useful purpose, the Germans still issued us with newspapers, one for the British and another for the Americans, even though we were now in the same compound.

It was a crude attempt to split the alliance between the two nations with the British version claiming that the Americans were sitting back and allowing the British to undertake all the dangerous missions; while the American edition would state the that it was the British who were sitting back.

Being together in the same compound, we obviously read each others' newspapers and they became a mockery, doing nothing to cause dissent between us as had been intended.

APPENDIX 1

Miscellaneous Correspondence

W. 22515/T12a 80,000 Pad 10/42 H.P 51-5583

R.A.F. Form 1924

POSTAGRAM.

Originator's Reference Number:-
BC/S.23197/P.

Date:— 8th October 1943.

To: P/O A. Bird (155025),
No.61 Squadron,
R.A.F.Station, Syerston.

From: The Commander-in-Chief, Bomber Command.

My warmest congratulations on the award of your

Distinguished Flying Cross.

A.T.Harris
Air Chief Marshal.

Originator's Signature		Time of Origin

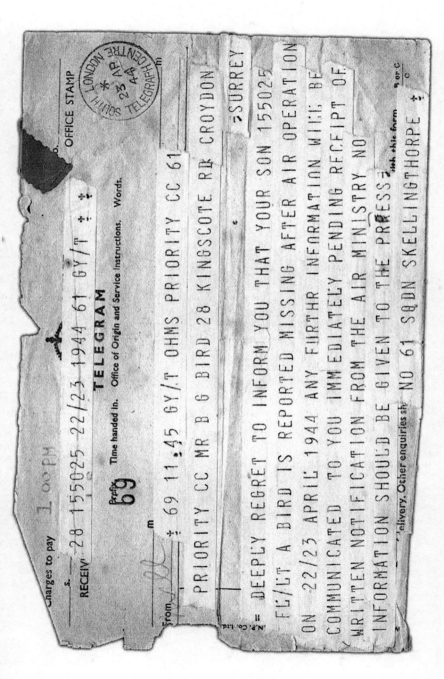

OFFICE STAMP

SOUTH LONDON TELEGRAPH CENTRE
23 AP 44

Charges to pay

£.

RECEIV— 28 155025 22/23 1944 61 GY/T ‡ ⁑

TELEGRAM

Prefix **69**   Time handed in.   Office of Origin and Service Instructions.   Words.

m

From

‡ 69 11.45 GY/T OHMS PRIORITY CC 61

PRIORITY CC MR B G BIRD 28 KINGSCOTE RD CROYDON

=SURREY

= DEEPLY REGRET TO INFORM YOU THAT YOUR SON 155025
FL/LT A BIRD IS REPORTED MISSING AFTER AIR OPERATION
ON 22/23 APRIL 1944 ANY FURTHR INFORMATION WILL BE
COMMUNICATED TO YOU IMMEDIATELY PENDING RECEIPT OF
WRITTEN NOTIFICATION FROM THE AIR MINISTRY NO
INFORMATION SHOULD BE GIVEN TO THE PRESS =
NO 61 SQDN SKELLINGTHORPE ⁑

delivery. Other enquiries sh...with this form

N.P. Co. Ltd.

Reference :
61S/1000/216/P.1.

No.61 Squadron,
Royal Air Force,
SKELLINGTHORPE,
Lincoln, Lincs.

25th April, 1944.

Dear Mr.Bird,

It is with the deepest regret that I have to confirm the news which you will have received by telegram, that your son Flight Lieutenant A.Bird, is missing with all his crew from air operations on the night of 22/23rd April, 1944.

He was detailed to attack Brunswick on that night, and, after the aircraft left this Station nothing more was heard of it. This in itself is not necessarily final, as wireless silence has to be maintained on operations to prevent the enemy from easily ascertaining the position and intention of our aircraft. There is therefore, every reasonable hope that he and his crew may have escaped by parachute, as so many others have done, in which case there should be good news of them. This news usually takes about six weeks to two months to come through, though the International Red Cross do all in their power to hasten news of prisoners-of-war. We must therefore hope and pray that there may soon be good news of your son and his crew.

Your son is a highly skilled Pilot, and this was his twenty third operational sortie, all the others having been highly successful. We also valued him as a fine type of Officer. His loss is a great blow to the Squadron.

The deep sympathy of all members of this Squadron is with you in this anxious time of waiting, which, we earnestly hope, will soon be happily terminated by good news.

It is desired to explain that the request in the telegram notifying you of the casualty to your son was included with the object of avoiding his chance of escape being prejudiced by undue publicity in case he was still at large. This is not to say that any information about him is available, but is a precaution adopted in the case of all personnel reported missing. Furthermore I would like to add that the names and addresses of the next-of-kin of the remainder of the crew cannot be given yet for reasons of security.

Yours very sincerely,

A.W.Doubleday

Mr.A.Bird,
28, Kingscote Road,
Croydon,
Surrey.

Wing Commander, Commanding,
No.61 Squadron.

Gerrard 9234.

Casualty Branch
77, Oxford Street
London, W.1.
1 May, 1944.

P.416262/1/P.4.A.2.

Sir,

I am commanded by the Air Council to express to you their great regret on learning that your son, Acting Flight Lieutenant Anthony Bird, D.F.C., Royal Air Force, is missing as the result of air operations on 23rd April, 1944, when a Lancaster aircraft in which he was flying as pilot set out to bomb Brunswick and failed to return.

This does not necessarily mean that he is killed or wounded, and if he is a prisoner of war he should be able to communicate with you in due course. Meanwhile enquiries are being made through the International Red Cross Committee, and as soon as any definite news is received you will be at once informed.

If any information regarding your son is received by you from any source you are requested to be kind enough to communicate it immediately to the Air Ministry.

The Air Council desire me to convey to you their sympathy in your present anxiety.

I am, Sir,

Your obedient Servant,

Charles Evans.

A.G. Bird, Esq.,
   28, Kingscote Road,
      Croydon,
         Surrey.

fell at *Linden*

TELEPHONE:
Gerrard 9234
HOLBORN 3484
Extn. 3801
Any communications on the
subject of this letter should
be addressed to:—

THE SECRETARY,

and the following number
quoted:—

P.416262/44/P.4.Cas.B3.

AIR MINISTRY,

LONDON, W.C.2.

(Casualty Branch),

73-77, Oxford Str

London, W.1.

P. to Thurnell

8 June, 1944.

Sir,

    I am directed to confirm a telegram from this department, in which
you were notified that information has now been received through the
International Red Cross Society stating that your son, Acting Flight
Lieutenant Anthony Bird D.F.C., Royal Air Force, is a prisoner of war a
a camp known as Stalag Luft 3 in Germany. Your son will now be able t
communicate direct to you.

    As no news has been received in respect of:-

2nd Pilot	J.10281	Flight Lieutenant H.C. Goodyear,
Navigator	169467	Pilot Officer F.J. Davis,
Wireless Operator	1388233	Sergeant B. Kenrick,
Mid Upper Gunner	1333458	Flight Sergeant R.V. George,
Engineer	171204	Pilot Officer R.H.P. Hollander,
Bomb aimer	144691	Flying Officer J.H. Pullman,
Rear Gunner	1101769	Flight Sergeant H. Aspinall, (D.F.M.)

other members of the crew reported missing with your son, you are
requested to be so good as to inform the Department of any information
relative to them received in letters from him.

    A pamphlet and handbook regarding communication with prisoner of w
are enclosed for your guidance.

        I am, Sir,
        Your obedient Servant,

        J.S. Shreeve

        for Director of Personal Service

A.G. Bird, Esq.,
  28, Kingscote Road,
    Croydon,
      Surrey.

POST � OFFICE TELEGRAM

c 28 77 PC 349 7/6/44 1707 B +

RECEIVED
at Central Telegraph
Office, E.C.1

Prefix. Time handed in. Office of Origin and Service Instructions.

OFFICE STAMP

HANDED IN

CROYDON SURREY 8 JUN 1944

From ___

To ___

7.30 [LONDON TELEX OHMS 53

PRIORITY GC A G BIRD ESQ 28 KINGSCOTE RD CROYDON =

FROM AIR MINISTRY 77 OXFORD ST PC 349 7/6/44

INFORMATION RECEIVED THROUGH THE INTERNATIONAL RED

CROSS COMMITTEE STATES THAT YOUR SON A/F/LT ANTHONY

BIRD DFC IS A PRISONER OF WAR IN GERMAN HANDS LETTER

CONFIRMING THIS TELEGRAM FOLLOWS HIS BROTHER IS

BEING INFORMED = 1707 B +

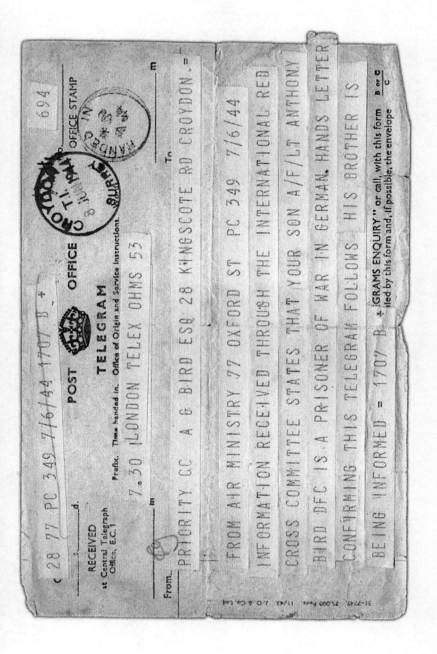

POST OFFICE

☩ TELEGRAM

Charges to pay

s. _____ d. _____

RECEIVED

From _____

Prefix. _____ Time handed in. _____ Office of Origin and Service Instructions. _____ Words. _____

9.28 m _____

OFFICE STAMP

CROYDON SURREY
8 JUN 44
T4

To _____

C CW FCGL 201 MEDICINE HAT 21 5

GLT MR AND MRS BIRD 28 KINGSCOTEROAD CROYDON SURRE

= YOUR LETTER CAME TODAYS TONYS CANADIAN FAMILY

MOURNS WITH YOU WRITING =

= MACCHARLES

For free repetition of doubtful words telephone "TELEGRAMS ENQUIRY," or call, with this form at office of delivery. Other enquiries should be accompanied by this form, and, if possible, the envelope.   B or C

(313267) Ho./80)

Telephone No.
SLOANE 9696

In replying please quote reference : PB/MP
RAF C.12198

7 BELGRAVE SQUARE,
LONDON, S.W.1

Mrs. Bird,
28, Kingscote Road,
CROYDON.

9th June. 1944.

Dear Mrs. Bird,

We have received your enquiry in
which you ask for news of your son, Acting
Flight Lieutenant A. Bird, D.F.C., No.
155025, Royal Air Force.

We are so sorry that we are not able
to give you any information about him at
present, but any news which may be forthcoming
from the International Red Cross Committee at
Geneva or from any other source will be
passed to you immediately. If, however, you
are the registered next of kin, your first
notification will come by telegram from the
Air Ministry.

May we say how much we sympathise
with you in your anxiety.

Yours sincerely,

Margaret Ampthill
Chairman.

MPB.

*When replying please
quote reference :—*
RAF/0/2405

**ST. JAMES'S PALACE,
LONDON, S.W.I**

A.G.Bird Esq.,
28,Kingscote Road,
Croyden,Surrey.

17th June,1944.

Dear Mr.Bird,

        F/Lieut. Anthony Bird.
    We are very glad to know that news
has been received of your son, and his
camp address has been noted in our records.
You will now be able to write to him,
directing your letters as follows:-

PRISONERS OF WAR POST
KRIEGSGEFANGENENPOST

155025,F/Lieut.Anthony Bird,
   British Prisoner of War,
      Stalag Luft lll,
         Germany.

    We understand that your son has not
yet been allotted a prisoner of war number, and until this has been received it
is not advisable to despatch any parcels,

                 P.T.O.

as this number is an added safeguard
to their delivery.   We think, however,
that you will shortly receive the number
from your son, and in the meantime we
are enclosing the next-of-kin parcel
label and clothing coupons, so that you
may prepare the first of these parcels
for posting later.

.   We also send you the leaflets   . .
PW/99C and PW/100A, which contain information
regarding letters and parcels for prisoners
of war which we think you will find of
interest.

We hope that if you have not already
heard from your son, you will do so in
the near future, and when you receive his
prisoner of war number we shall be glad
if you will notify this Office.

Yours sincerely,

p.p. E. M. THORNTON.

Director.

Reference :
61S/1000/216/P.1.

No.61 Squadron,
Royal Air Force,
SKELLINGTHORPE,
Lincoln, Lincs.

19th June, 1944.

Dear Mr.Bird,

     Many thanks for your letter of the 12th June. We are all very glad to know that you have heard from Tony and that he is unharmed and cheerful. Knowing him, I am sure that he will keep his chin up and help his companions to do the same. He certainly must have had a miraculous escape. It will be grand to hear his story from him personally when he gets back home which, we hope, will be soon! Have you his Prisoner of War number, as some of his friends would like to write to him? When you write, please tell him that all his friends are delighted to hear that he is safe and well, and wish him a speedy return home.

     I am having him enrolled as a member of the Caterpillar Club. The membership card and emblem will be sent direct to you.

     As regards his car, this is quite safe. It cannot be released to you without Air Ministry authority, but application for this is being made, so that you may remove the car if you wish. As soon as authority is obtained, you will be notified, and I think it would then be advisable for you to have the car.

     I have no news yet of the rest of Tony's crew, but we still hope to hear that they are safe.

Yours sincerely,

A.Doubleday.

Wing Commander, Commanding,
No.61 Squadron.

Mr.A.G.Bird,
28, Kingscote Road,
CROYDON,
Surrey.

RAF/O/2405

...ANISATION

of the

BRITISH RED CROSS SOCIETY and ORDER OF ST. JOHN OF JERUSALEM

PRISONERS OF WAR DEPARTMENT.

Chairman :

MAJOR-GENERAL SIR RICHARD HOWARD-VYSE, K.C.M.G., D.S.O.

Deputy Chairman :

General Manager of Packing Centres :　**SIR MONTAGUE EDDY, C.B.E.**　　*Directors :*

THE LORD REVELSTOKE　　　　　　　　　　　　　　**LT.-COL. M. W. BROWN, O.B.E.**

MISS E. M. THORNTON, O.B.E.

TELEPHONE NO. :
ABBEY 5841

When replying please quote reference—　RAF/O/2405
RBR/LELJ.

ST. JAMES'S PALACE,

LONDON, S.W.1

11th September, 1944.

Mrs. A.G.Bird,
28, Kingscote Road,
Croydon, Surrey.

Dear Mrs. Bird,

Ft/Lt. Anthony Bird.

Thank you for your letter of September 5th and we are so sorry to learn that you have been worried about your son. We are afraid that the delay in the delivery of mail has been very general and the majority of relatives of R.A.F. prisoners of war have not had letters dated later than in April or early May.

We know how very much you must look forward to having more news, but we do hope you will not be unduly anxious if you do not receive a letter for some time, as very considerable delays must be expected in the coming weeks.

With regard to parcels, the situation is still unchanged and no useful purpose will be served in forwarding any more to your son as they are not leaving this country at the

CENTRAL CHANCERY OF
THE ORDERS OF KNIGHTHOOD,
St JAMES'S PALACE, S.W.1.

28th November, 1945.

Sir,

  The King will hold an Investiture at Buckingham Palace on Tuesday, the 11th December, 1945, at which your attendance is requested.

  It is requested that you should be at the Palace not later than 10.15 o'clock a.m. (Doors open at 9.45 a.m.)

    DRESS:-Service Dress; Morning Dress; Civil Defence
      Uniform or Dark Lounge Suit.

  This letter should be produced by you on entering the Palace, as no further card of admission will be issued.

  I am desired to inform you that you may be accompanied by two relations or friends to witness the Investiture, but I regret that owing to the limited accommodation available for spectators, it is not possible for this number to be increased. The spectators' tickets may be obtained on application to this Office and I have to ask you, therefore, to complete the enclosed form and return it to me immediately.

    I am, Sir,

      Your obedient Servant,

        Gockley.

         Secretary.

Flight Lieutenant Anthony Bird,
    D.F.C., R.A.F.V.R.

APPENDIX 2

Jock Reid VC

REID, William, VC – Flight Lieutenant, No. 61 Squadron, Royal Air Force Volunteer Reserve.

On the night of 3rd/4th November, 1943, 344 Lancasters, 233 Halifaxes and 12 Mosquitoes, went on the Dusseldorf raid. The main raid fell on the centre and south of the city. This was the first large scale test of the G-H blind-bombing device attempting to bomb the Mannesmann tubular-steel works. Bomber Command used 38 Lancasters for this test. Only 15 aircraft bombed the factory successfully. Flight Lieutenant Reid was flying a Lancaster in this operation. Thirty miles inside the Dutch coast, on the outward leg, his aircraft LM360 "O" was attacked by a German Me110, night fighter and a few minutes later by a German FW190. Despite severe damage to the aircraft , his Navigator being killed, the Wireless Operator also fatally wounded, the Engineer having a broken arm, himself wounded in the head, arms, hand and shoulder, and then showered with broken glass and perspex, as the windshield was smashed by bullets, Reid continued on to the target and made his bombing run. He then managed to fly back to his base, when upon landing his undercarriage collapsed.

Flight Lieutenant Reid was awarded with a Victoria Cross for his conspicuous gallantry and devotion to duty in carrying out this operation to a successful conclusion.

He recovered from his injuries to fly again, this time in No. 617 Squadron, bringing with him two of his crew. On the last day of 1944, 617 Squadron went to Rilly la Montagne, which was a bomb storage depot, in limestone caves, near Rheims. Two Mosquitos and 16 Lancasters took off. Over the target Reid made his bombing run and was turning away when his Bomb-aimer said "Hold it, hold it." Reid had to hold for the bombing pictures to be taken. Then behind him he heard crashing sounds coming from his aircraft. He knew that in loose formation there was always the possibility of another aircraft higher up dropping it's bombs on the 'plane below. It had happened many times to other pilots; this time it had happened to his own aircraft. One of these bombs had torn through the fuselage, damaging the rudder controls. After the first bump, Reid ordered the crew to prepare to bale out of the aircraft. After the second bump he gave the order to bale out. His Engineer, called Stewart, handed Reid his parachute, but by this time the aircraft had began to spin out of control. Fighting the G-forces, he struggled to get out through the 'dinghy hatch' in the roof. He suceeded, and hit a tree on landing, fortunately not injuring himself too badly. As he found his feet, he was able to move off in a southerly direction, using his escape map, knowing that he was about 30 miles from Paris. However, a forceful challenge from three German soldiers with bayonets fixed changed his mind. As Reid was marched away and saw the tailplane of his crashed Lancaster and asked if anyone else was alive from his crew. There were two of his crew still in the wreckage. The tail-gunner and another of his crew was in the tail section of the aircraft. He was able to inform the Germans who these men were, so that the next of kin could be informed. Reid was then taken to a small flak site and attended to by a doctor. About twenty minutes later his Wireless Operator was brought in limping. They were the only two survivors of the crash. On his way to prisoner of war camp, a German in Brussels noticed Reid's VC ribbon and said in German "Knight's Cross".

Flight Lieutenant Reid survived the War and was repatriated home as a POW.

William Reid was born in Glasgow, Scotland on 21st December, 1921. He is still alive in the year 2000.

The above is an extract from *Victoria Cross: Bravest of the Brave*, a comprehensive listing of every Victoria Cross gallantry award during the 19th and 20th centuries, compiled by A.E Horsman and published by Woodfield.